Advance Praise for *What an MBA Taught Me...But My Kids Made Me Learn*

"With humor and wisdom, *What an MBA Taught Me...* shows us how family and work life actually benefit each other, and how to truly embrace resilience, risk, and authenticity."

—Dorie Clark, author of *Reinventing You*,
executive education faculty, Duke
University Fuqua School of Business

"As a working mother and HBS alum, I loved Bea's insightful take on the value of parenting skills in the business world. Lots of laugh out loud stories mixed in with proven, practical advice."

—Lynn Vojvodich, Member, Board of
Directors, Ford Motor Company

"Bea Wray is an incredible storyteller and excellent source of inspiration. So much of *What an MBA Taught Me...* resonated deeply with me: embracing the imposter syndrome, reframing 'I haven't done that yet,' not letting parenting be a smudge on your resume...just to name a few."

—Sameera Bazaz, Chief Strategy Officer,
The Hot Mommas Project

"Bea Wray's story-telling technique is gripping. Being 700k in debt, moving to an island with a few hundred residents, raising three kids on her own, moving to Australia...are just a few stories of risk-taking that show what resilience looks like, and why LOVE makes it work. In Bea's book, she empowers readers to take risks and live authentically, with love."

—Amy C. Edmondson, Professor, Harvard Business School, author of *The Fearless Organization*

"With raw wit, Bea Wray shares how it's possible to Go Big AND Go Home. *What an MBA Taught Me...* humorously shatters the myth of work-life balance and gives us all the confidence to embrace our true value. Highly recommended!"

—Linda Rottenberg, Co-Founder & CEO, Endeavor; author of *NYT* bestseller *Crazy Is a Compliment*

"I've always been a passionate believer in work-life integration so I figured I would nod my head throughout the book, relating. Instead I found myself experiencing refreshing insights and inspirational nuggets that I can easily apply, all made more real by the shared laughs and humility. A great read for any business leader and parent (or even if you're just one of them!)."

—Tara Walpert Levy, VP of Agency and Brand Solutions, Google

"Bea's uplifting words encourage me to continue to integrate all areas of my life. I believe more business executives should follow Bea's raw and meaningful leadership advice. This book reminds us of the power of Authenticity and helps a leader develop from a good leader into a great one."

—Carolin Archibald, President & CEO, Ameda, Inc.

What an MBA Taught Me...

BUT
MY KIDS
MADE ME
LEARN

BEA WRAY

Post Hill
PRESS

A POST HILL PRESS BOOK
ISBN: 978-1-64293-707-7
ISBN (eBook): 978-1-64293-708-4

What an MBA Taught Me...
But My Kids Made Me Learn

Cover photo and author photos by Keith Morgan (photographer) and Juwan Platt (producer)
Illustrations by Jess Telmanik

Post Hill Press
New York • Nashville
posthillpress.com

Published in the United States of America
1 2 3 4 5 6 7 8 9 10

Table of Contents

Foreword

by Rerai Albaugh

Bea and I moved to a remote bridgeless island on the same day. That experience shaped my life in delightful and unimaginable ways. So, I get the honor of writing this book's foreword because your life is about to change in delightful and unimaginable ways too!

I sat in a near meditative state as the boat rocked slowly, gliding across the Calibogue Sound. Out of the blue, a beautiful lady in athletic clothing bounded towards me. "Hi, I'm Bea, I'm moving to Daufuskie today and we are going to be great friends."

Meditation over...a new life begins!

Bea and I raised our children together, reveling in the brief but spectacular opportunity to immerse them in wildlife, Gullah history, and unique island culture. Bea was different. A different kind of woman and a different kind of mom. Where I might exercise early in the morning and "get cleaned up for the day," Bea moved all day long. In one day, she would play tennis, set up crab traps off the dock, ride bikes to the school and back, teach German to the seventeen island students, conduct a few meetings, and love her husband. It was exhausting to watch and yet inspiring.

Previously, my professional career had included time on AirForce Two amongst world leaders. Yet, surprisingly, it was on a remote island where I was learning and growing even moreso.

From Bea, I learned incredible business insights that she gleaned during her time owning a high-tech company and attending Harvard Business School. She had an uncanny ability to effectively use the skills for managing teams to manage her life. For example, her children baked their own cupcakes for the school party, instead of buying them as I did. Those kids had ownership over their lives from an early age.

Bea also knew how to make anything happen. I recall when she received an invitation for a wedding in Austria. At that time, Bea was a stay at home mom and was living very modestly. Her husband said, "There is no way we can go to this wedding." Bea's response, which slayed me, was "Honey, there's no way we *can't* go." She bartered flight mileage points, exchanged homes, and who knows what else. She and her children enjoyed a splendid month in Austria. Bea looked like Maria Von Trapp as she rambled across mountains in her green dirndl with three children and a tuba.

However, things got hard. I watched her go back to a failing marriage four times while financial devastation ensued. Life got real so Bea got writing.

That writing planted the seeds of this book. Bea dug deep to expose the underpinnings of her superpowers. Mastering things like gratitude, resilience, efficiency, and a positive attitude allowed her to thrive, turning trials into triumph. These

lessons and more come to life in *What an MBA Taught Me...
But My Kids Made Me Learn.* I relish in re-learning them
while reading Bea's beautifully written stories. So will you!

Your professional and personal lives are about to journey
to new heights. This book is Bea, bounding up to you to say,
"We're going to be great friends!"

—*Renai Albaugh*

Introduction

"I'm from wherever you are." Honest...well, sorta. The two common questions people tend to ask when introducing one another other are "What's your name?" and "Where are you from?" So, they seem like logical kick-off questions as you and I stand in this bookstore aisle deciding whether we are going to take this relationship to the next level.

To be fair, you are the one standing. I am just sitting. Over here...in the coffee shop. The one with an almond milk latte motioning for you to bring along the book and come join me.

I can barely wait to hear your answers to the questions. To the first I answer, "Bea Wray," which sounds like Bee-Ray. You can call me Bea, Dee, Bee-A, or Bay. I don't really care as long as you call me. More than one giggle has erupted when my pals text me and spellcheck converts my name to "Bra," so in certain contexts that is acceptable too. The *W* in Wray is silent, but I am called "Ms. Wary" way more often than I am called "Ms. Ray."

Siri has her own version too. Siri is in the business of AI (artificial intelligence). I am a motivational speaker. Yet lately I wonder if she is encroaching on my turf. She calls me

Be-A-Ray. Like she wants me to be a ray of sunshine. So that is what I am committed to doing for you. If you will join me on this adventure, I promise to brighten your day.

So where are you from, anyway? My standard answer: "I am from wherever you are!" I grew up in thirteen homes across America as my father climbed the Ford Motor Company ladder throughout various manufacturing plants (yes, those existed in the US in the seventies and eighties).

When I turned eighteen, I inquired with a local official, "Hi, in which state should I register to vote?"

"Where do you live?" she asked with a smirk as if my question were absurd.

"Well, my parents live here in South Carolina, but I attend college in Georgia."

"Oh, in which state is your driver's license?" she continued, believing the answer will break the tie.

"New Jersey," I responded, "that is where I had graduated high school."

"Uh, okay," she slowed down a bit as if to validate my confusion. "Well, where will you be during the election?"

I breathed in, happy she hadn't given up on me (yet). "England," I muttered, barely able to look up at her, "I am taking a year abroad."

That situation made me realize that I am really not like everyone else. My entire life has been a constant crash course in people skills. As a result, I feel "at home" in many places. My stories and encouragement will feel "at home" swaying in your hammock or as you multitask on your stationary bicycle. Won't you please take them there?

Due to selling a company, I was afforded the privilege of taking six years off from the corporate grind in order to be at home with my children. When it was time to return to the workforce, I felt intimidated and lacked confidence. I wondered what expertise I could bring to the table, and I worried it would be difficult to secure and succeed in meaningful and financially rewarding assignments.

To my delight, my career took off. I was happier, more impactful, and more successful than I ever had been. I constantly heard, "Wow, thank you! You have changed my business." The role was to direct community non-profit economic development and support hundreds of entrepreneurs. I wondered, what skill do I have that is helping these people achieve their goals? The second question was more important. Where did I get those skills?

Amazingly, the answer wasn't mostly from attending a prestigious business school. Further, it wasn't mostly because I had been an entrepreneur for nearly twenty years. Rather, upon reflection, I realized that the competence fueling my success (expertise in collaboration, focus, strategic planning, communication, and so on) were all skills I honed predominantly through motherhood.

Simply put, business is done with people, so people skills matter. That's the real differentiator in the business world—how well are you able to get along with others, motivate them, serve with them, team up with them, support them, lead them, and above all, bring out the best in them? For me, a great place to master people skills is to try to raise some people in the home, where the stakes are high!

I don't want to shortchange Harvard, quite the opposite. Harvard Business School does a phenomenal job of creating environments which encourage students to improve their all-important people savvy. Emphasizing relationship building early in the application process, assigning a workload that requires the formation of study groups, and an intense and active classroom inspiring impeccable listening skills are only a few examples of how the school organizes the educational experience specifically to teach incredible people ingenuity. In this book, you and I will journey together through the MBA experience. We will dive into the most significant lessons taught there.

Harvard is renowned for its commitment to the case study method. There are no lectures or scripted lessons. Rather, professors are required to be facilitators, devil's advocates, listeners, moderators, and hosts. They manage discussions around real-life protagonists and challenges so that classmates can analyze, compare, and grow from experiences as if they have lived it themselves.

You have heard of OPM—Other People's Money—and I am guessing if you have ever taken out a loan or had a mortgage, you are grateful to have been able to tap some OPM. Similarly,

I love the method of teaching OPM—Other People's Mistakes. I want you to achieve great things and fulfill your dreams. You don't have to slog through your full lifespan to gain a lifetime's worth of experience. In the spirit of the case method, this book is chock full of real-life professional stories from personal experiences as an entrepreneur combined with my twenty years as a leader, mentor, and investor to over three hundred startup companies.

Similarly, dividing the class into sections was a hallmark of my MBA experience. For example, I was in Section J, the best one (*wink*—we all think ours was best). Thus, for the first year, we had all our classes, and much of our social lives, with only our section. Eighty people started to feel more like an intimate gathering of our closest friends.

If you are not yet convinced you need this book for you and your dreams, how about giving it a go for those around you? In 2013, Sheryl Sandberg rejected the notion that careers are linear corporate ladders. She introduced the concept that careers are more akin to jungle gyms and thus benefit from a wider variety of experiences. It breaks my heart that often parenting is treated like a black smudge, something to be hidden from—not highlighted on—a LinkedIn profile or resume. Will you help me with one specific goal of this book? That is to secure parenting as a valid position upon the career jungle gym.

I know the power of declaring the truth...even before it happens...especially before it happens. So, here I go. This book will equip you with a full range of people skills that will transform your career and make you more effective, successful, and yes, happier in your workplaces. Moms, you will read this book and discover a newfound sense of respect for the laborious tasks parenting entails and the positive outcomes you are creating in your children.

Dads, if you picked up this book for your wife or daughter—great! Thanks for caring about her in such a profound way. Now, please read on. Not for her but for yourself. The wisdom in these pages is relevant to your career too. This book gives you the best of what you might be taught in a top business program, and it helps you understand the aspects of parenting that can be applied in other settings.

Mostly, this book is for you if you are ready to succeed. Are you tired of feeling pulled in too many directions? Annoyed that your energies seem to spin uselessly? Are your dreams buried rather than blossoming?

Then it is time for you and I to laugh together. We might cry together too. We will certainly grow into better versions of ourselves.

I have carefully selected and perfected my best stories, tips, tricks, and advice for extraordinary leaders and parents. They now fill the pages of the book in your hands, ready to help your goals rise like the morning sun into realities.

If you are committed to hanging on tight to your mommy guilt, then this book is not for you. Please slip it back on the shelf and trade it in for some impossible craft manual or complicated recipe book designed to make you (and me) feel like we are not good enough.

Alternatively, if you are ready to let go of self-limiting habits and what Rachel Hollis correctly deems "a special kind of oppression," then do it. Hand in your victim card and stomp out your mommy guilt. Start recognizing that your job raising children is jam packed with experiences, lessons, and stories that are improving your abilities to direct and guide.

So, if you are the expert (and you are), then why read a book by me? Good question. Perhaps this is where I am supposed to tell you how I graduated at the top of my class from Harvard, sold a company for millions of dollars, and raised perfect children. Not so fast. I promise, I will share those stories in detailed (and surprising) ways through the pages of this book. For now, however, as I vie for this book to earn its rightful spot on your nightstand, I want to speak about two things: love and children.

My greatest pet peeve is when someone calls me "smart." It is not that I think I am dumb. I just don't want anyone to minimize my oversized heart. I have a true and deep desire for you to succeed. Any intellect I have is the direct result of my devotion to figuratively and literally stand too close to ledges, roll down hills, and climb mountains in hopes that I am helping someone else. Think Labrador Retriever.

Don't believe me? I make my living as a keynote and motivational speaker. Being an author and a speaker is in itself an oxymoron. One requires me to be an introvert, thriving in alone time. The other requires me to be an extravert, eager to welcome the warm embrace of strangers. I wonder how many trapeze artists are afraid of heights.

Children motivate. Mine tease, "Harvard is probably some small town in rural Georgia." Thus, it is logical that I went there at some point. They are not being disrespectful, just real.

I was hired once to help a company raise revenue from roughly $10 million in annual sales to $100 million annually. We expected growth to take a few years. The company was located two hours away. Right away, I made a decision for my children to stay with my sister for a few weeks until we could move to Charleston as a family. The first week, I toiled for eleven hours each day at the office. In the evenings, I explored neighborhoods, schools, and rental homes. Friday afternoon, I drove the two-hour commute to see my children. Boy, I was spent! My daughter Savannah had recently received her driver's license, so luckily, she was eager to drive me the final hour to our resting place for the evening. I stretched back in the car and my eyelids slowly shut. I felt the car slide back in reverse. *Ahhh, peace.* All of a sudden, the car jerked into park. I looked up, thinking, "What's happening here?"

Savannah turned to me and said, "Mom, you were hired to take the company from ten million to one hundred million over a three-year period. You've been there for a week. Did you get to eleven yet?"

Children! They teach us. They challenge us. This book isn't about lying back in the passenger seat. Hold on to your copy, strap on your seat belt, and let's go for a powerful ride.

Note:

I like games, expanding our minds, and sharing my life with my kids. For example, if I were in the process of purchasing a home you might find me scribbling down a word search for my kids. It would include terms like mortgage, interest rate, down payment, etc.

So, please consider the illustrations at the beginning of each section as an invitation to play along. Enjoy!

Part 1

Purpose Equals People

Turns Out "Soft" Skills Are Pretty Hard

• Go for It •

• Things Aren't Always As They Seem •

• Embracing Failure, Failure Can Be Fabulous •

SOEPPRU —> PURPOSE

ADHR —> HARD

OFTS —> SOFT

SLILKS —> SKILLS

REAFLIU —> FAILURE

BCREEMA —> EMBRACE

ASFLUUBO —> FABULOUS

Chapter 1

Go for It!

This first chapter is called "Go for It!" for a reason.

Let's do this thing.

Your thing.

The dream, idea, new product, or venture you have been putting off. Let's do it! Let's go for it.

Are you ready?

As you read this paragraph, pause and close your eyes for just a minute. See yourself as you purchased this book. You may have been at one of my workshops and were inspired by my story. You may have heard about it from a friend or seen it on Amazon. Think about why you purchased this book and what you want to take from it. You've got a desire to go further in your life. So, let's go! You picked up the book for a reason, so let's get started.

Let's talk about stretching our comfort zones. What lofty ambitions are you considering? I want them in your heart and mind now, right now, right here. Please hold open these decisions (if you are like me that is literally, at least for a moment, holding out your hands, palms up) and let the pages of this book fill you with encouragement, advice, stories, laughter, and an impetus to *take...this...step*!

To get the ball rolling I am offering you three stories of big risks I took. The stories foreshadow the contextual map of this book. I view them from the three essential lenses of my life: business school, "real world" professional experience, and parenting.

Risk One: Applying to Harvard Business School

Initially, B-school was the farthest thing from my mind. In my early years, I intended to study psychology and was singularly driven towards a lifetime of analysis and experimentation in this realm. I woke up early every Saturday morning, and instead of watching cartoons like a normal child, I enthusiastically watched Dr. Brazelton talk about child behavior. I attended Emory University and intended on applying to psychology graduate school. Lucky me, I connected with a great advisor early on and had excellent grades, so I was invited to do an honors thesis. The idea of the thesis research excited me, but I found I immensely disliked the experience. I detested how inconclusive it was. I despised how I needed more and more data to ensure that my control group was large enough or that my conclusions were reliable. I abhorred how hard I had to work for six months to only conclude nothing at all or "the evidence is not sufficient."

I studied the cross-modality theory of dyslexia, which in itself was kind of cool. The theory was (and is) that normal readers hear themselves as they read. Envision that the words "cross" from the visual mode to the auditory mode. This theory purports that it is in this crossing of modalities that many dyslexics struggle. The Stroop test is a color and word test basically measuring cognitive interference of a second stimulus. For my study, I gave a control group of normal readers and a test group of dyslexic readers three timed tests. The first was hundreds of colored ovals which the subject had to identify ("red, blue, red, yellow," and so on). The second was words of the names of colors written out in black ink which the subjects had to read (again, something like: "red, yellow, blue, blue"). Finally, each person was timed identifying the color of the ink which was spelling the name of a different color (for example for the word "blue" written in red ink, the subject would say "red"). When normal readers take these three tests the results are basically fast, fast, slow. When hearing-impaired individuals take these three tests the results are basically fast, fast, fast. I theorized that dyslexics might (like the hearing impaired) test fast, fast, fast. If that were true, then we would have more insight as to specifically teaching them how to read.

I loved the questions and potential impact, but I really hated that so many had to be this age or that, left-handed or not, on and on. I realized I could have studied anything and been similarly frustrated as I failed to deliver conclusive evidence. Initially, I thought, "I flunked at this level, but grad school will be great."

So, tail between my legs, I strode into my honors thesis defense presentation and faced the four intimidating advisors. I presented my study and results (or lack thereof) for nearly two hours. I gave up any hope of graduating with high or highest honors and just wanted some acknowledgement of all the work. I concluded my presentation and answered their questions before I waited for them to ponder the results and deliver what I was certain would be bad news.

Much to my surprise, my thesis earned a summa cum laude grade, the highest honors! Thrilling! At first. I later reflected on it all, and I had an unexpected reaction. I thought, *If this inconclusive work is a success, then I don't want it.* I cancelled my arrangements to spend a year in my advisor's research laboratory.

That same week, I was invited to have lunch with an entrepreneur, and before lunch ended, he offered me a sales position in his company. It was graduation weekend. In four hours, I would be having a celebratory dinner with my parents and extended family. I envisioned hugging them and thanking them profusely for the gobs of money they had poured into my tuition the past four years and the endless encouragement and support they had offered for the late-night studying. Then I imagined telling them, *I don't know what it was all for, and I have no plan.*

I accepted the offer even though I had no clue about the field, sales, or office environments. I simply knew dinner would taste better if I had a post-graduation plan.

I quickly found I loved business! I loved that our goals were clearly set, and we knew when we succeeded or failed. I thrived working closely with other people. The fast-paced entrepreneurial environment and the autonomy of sales energized me.

Looking back, I should have known entrepreneurship was in my genes. As an eight-year-old, I delivered newspapers, babysat, walked dogs, and mowed lawns. By twelve, I started a newsletter business, and by fourteen, I was paid to iron men's dress shirts. I did not think of those activities as work or innovation, or commerce, but they were. I wasn't even terribly motivated to earn money; I just sort of did the next thing. One day, I got scolded by my mom. "Bea," she said, "you have got to stop all these odd jobs. The neighbors are bringing bags of apples because they think dad has been fired and we must be hard up for cash." I didn't stop.

Selling allowed me to see the intricacies of companies. I often peered into a new company each day. I met new impressive professionals. Mostly, I relished setting specific goals and achieving them. One product I sold sparked the creation of new products which lead to the establishment of a whole new division, a West Coast office, and eventually two new companies. By age twenty-seven, I became a CEO of a Silicon Valley high tech company with more than thirty employees. Yes, I liked business! As all of this happened, I started to think about going to business school. I frequently met people who had MBAs, and I was impressed with how articulate and confident they were.

I decided to apply. **Here is the lesson**. If you asked me whether I thought it was likely I would get accepted, I would have said not only "no" but "hell no!" **Often the secret to making a big stride is to not think about the likely outcome, just make the move anyway.** For me it was just one more "sales" call. As any decent salesperson, I was strategic, and I made two decisions.

First, I chose Harvard. Sure, it has a stellar reputation and powerful network, but many schools have that. When I chose to apply to Harvard Business School, it was the only school I applied to because it was the only school in the country that did not require the GMAT (Graduate Management Admission Test). I was afraid of the GMAT. So, that was one hurdle I didn't have to face.

Second, I read the brochure, which highlighted teams and building relationships. I grew up in thirteen homes across five states, so I knew a thing or two about making friends and building relationships. Additionally, the admissions team was clear that they sought people who specifically targeted their MBA program. I even read (or dreamed up) that if you apply the second year in a row (after getting rejected the previous year), you will increase your likelihood of being accepted.

So, I threw in an application a year earlier than I hoped to really apply, sort of just to "prime the pump." Do you know what Delta Dash is? That's when you not only wait till the last day, but the last minute. Delta Dash was for those of us who missed the 5:00 p.m. FedEx pickup. I was attending a ski vacation/conference in Utah, which luckily is a Delta hub. I had until 9:30 PM to rush this "primer" application to the airport and still have it arrive by the morning deadline in Boston. I call it a "primer" application because I didn't care if anyone even read it and it never crossed my mind that I might get admitted. I just wanted to check the box that I had submitted an application which I believed would help me the following year. Crazy thing. *I got accepted.*

Risk Two: Selling a Company

In 2005, I was running a small company that was (after a very slow start) doing reasonably well. We were barely profitable, finally making payroll consistently, and we were expanding. We had an excellent reputation and dominant brand recognition in the teensy niche market of software escrow. Our company, SourceHarbor, helped corporations license software by serving as a neutral third party that held onto the source code, the recipe of the software. In the event the software developer defaulted on support or went out of business, we would operate under specific and strict contractual language to release the source code to the licensee so that they could continue to utilize the software. So we were insurance for large software purchasers, and we were marketing and sales assistance for software developers. It was in facilitating the growth of these cutting-edge companies that I caught the start-up bug and cut my teeth with innovative industries.

Fortunately, we also served huge companies like Abbott Laboratories and Coca-Cola, who licensed tons of software from a variety of vendors. So we invested heavily in acquiring those key customers and then worked for the business to catch up with that investment. We were steady, but we were nowhere near a position to think about an exit.

On November 1, I received a phone call from an investment banker. At this point, I had two young children and a third one on the way. The baby was due at Thanksgiving. On the call, the investment banker informed me about a competitor out in California. I'd never heard of this company because it didn't have a great market presence. They stopped investing any money into marketing, which meant their growth slowed, yet their profitability soared to 90 percent. Wow! The investment banker informed me that the deal had to close by December 31.

As he spoke, I glanced at photographs of my toddlers and thought, *They're expecting stockings, Christmas, Santa...you know, the works.* I didn't know anything about buying an existing company, but I knew one thing for sure: this fella was not a parent. If he were, there is no logical way he would continue barking up my tree and bother to ask as he did, "Do you want to buy the company?"

I heard, "Sure!"

I looked around my tiny office wondering who had just spoken. To my horror, I realized it was *me*!

Of course it was me. I was going to go for it! We were barely making it...but we *were making it*. So I attempted to buy the company.

I circled back with some of my original investors, who were now super happy with our progress. They brought on some partners and we put together a few-million-dollar bid for this company. I knew exactly what it was worth because I'd been in this industry and knew exactly what every contract was worth. We had two United States rivals. Similarly, they put together their bids. And what was super interesting was all of us were submitting almost the exact same amount.

But I'm supposed to tell you a story about selling, not a story about purchasing a company.

The bids went in, and we lost. None of the three leading companies won because our amounts were too low. Our presentation told a convincing narrative about how we had the most respectable brand and the most impressive and widespread customer base. My submission described how the marriage between our reputation and expansion combined with their solid client roster and profit was sure to succeed. I worked hard to paint the vision because some aspect of our proposal was a performance-based buyout, and I needed the narrative to illustrate how the payout would be secure.

However, again, we did not win the bid. A fourth unanticipated contestant from the UK won. This was 2005 and the pound sterling was very strong at that time. In fact, it had just spiked, so it was as if they were playing with Monopoly money. They came in at about a 40 percent increase from the three other bids. Clearly, it was a no-brainer.

Here is a great lesson: it's important to know not only where you are and where you're going, but what's around you, like dollar value versus another currency. Correspondingly, as I mentor young adults, we attempt to examine the atmosphere around their decisions. For example, some have lamented to me that it must be a difficult time to find employment. Their evidence for this was that they had submitted two resumes to no avail. Then we researched together that the current unemployment rate was only 2 percent, and I recounted memories of living through unemployment rates that were 20 percent. So, if this heft feels like pressure now, imagine it ten times worse. They made the wise decision of working a bit harder to secure a position.

It is not all about working harder. Times with a low unemployment rate are ideal for stretching towards opportunities for which you might not have full qualifications. Paying attention to the financial environment matters.

In the situation with my attempt to purchase a company, it was the story, not the dollar value that changed my life. Indeed, we would be an exemplary partner. That truth was so compelling that by January, the buyer from England who just secured the purchase of my California competitor turned around and wanted to buy us too.

I took a big leap to buy a company and went for it. The result was incredible—within six months I sold my company at an overpriced valuation during a precarious time. This transition allowed me to dedicate the next six years to the joy of raising three children.

Side note: I even had a chance to enlarge the payout. Most of our contracts lasted eight years. So for every dollar of revenue, I received an eight times multiple for the price of the company.

I had twelve more months to sell new deals and I'd get eight dollars for every one dollar of revenue that I acquired.

Tara Sophia Mohr begins her 2014 *Harvard Business Review* article, "You've probably heard the following statistic: Men apply for a job when they meet only 60% of the qualifications, but women apply only if they meet 100% of them." I had almost none of the skills I thought were necessary for success to buy that company, but we raised our hand anyway. I hope you will consider doing the same next time opportunity knocks.

Risk Three: Moving Family to a Bridgeless Island

Following the sale of SourceHarbor, we moved to paradise. Literally. If you are searching for Daufuskie Island, South Carolina on a map, I suggest looking right next to Heaven.

You and I live in a world where opinions abound about literally every aspect of our lives. Someone wants to tell you where your children should go to school, how and when they should play travel sports, at what age music lessons and foreign language are a must, how much kale you need to eat, and how weight training is better than cardio. The most important takeaway from this book: *you* and *you alone* know what is best for you and your career and your children. Sure, learn constantly and be open, but please, please, please trust your instincts.

As a new parent, I felt overwhelmed by cultural demands. I sensed an overbearing pressure to do things that didn't sit well with me: organized sports for four-year-olds, overscheduled children, uninspired TV with lame content, handheld game devices, and much more. I felt terrified by huge schools and those dreaded long car lines. I wanted quiet and nature. Where could I find that?

While b-school showed me that *going for it* has benefits, and my career illustrated *going for it* can pay off, my kids motivated me to *go for it* by making an even more important decision.

After I sold the company, I went against all the social norms and well-meaning advice. We moved to Daufuskie Island where we lived for six glorious years. Our children were three of only seventeen in the entire school. For years, I introduced my son Robert saying something like, "This is Robert, the smartest kid in the second grade."

He would smile and add, "And the dumbest." He was the *only* child in his grade.

On this remote island, we faithfully attended the African Baptist Church, which sometimes was rocking with southern hymns and other days had four people in the pews due to rain and muddy dirt roads travelled only by slow golf carts.

It was a plunge for sure to buck the system (not to mention the advice of my mother-in-law's pals who had educated their own kids in expensive, exclusive private schools). In the six years, thirty or more couples sought our advice as they were attempting to also move to the island. Inevitably, either the husband or the wife was desperate for the move but never able to convince the other. They just couldn't let go of this quick and easy visit to Target, Walgreens, and the like—the very things I was determined to escape. Honest to goodness, I once ran into the ladies' room at Target as I felt the flu coming on. My poor young daughter was convinced for years that I was allergic to such stores.

Talking to these many couples, I made an important observation. Most people are willing to dream and consider adding on to their lives. However, they are more reluctant to let go of aspects of life as they know it. This is true even when they realize that the thing they are holding onto is the very thing keeping them from their dream.

On Daufuskie, our typical day included Robert at age four riding the extend-a-bike, while toddler William was bumped up and down the handlebar baby carrier. We arrived at school on time to join the sixteen other students for a lunch carefully prepared by our Gullah buddy who was a second mother to each of the children, all from widely varying backgrounds. Robert remained for preschool, and William and I rode back, stopping at the community farm to milk a goat or to the beach to hunt for treasures. Worth the gamble? Am I happy I went for it? You betcha!

Nevertheless, me and my adventures are not what is relevant. We're here to talk about you! Let's revisit those goals, challenges, and advances you are considering or delaying, and let's get going.

Chapter 2

Things Aren't Always
As They Seem

Parenting *seems* irrelevant to business, but *is* it? Things aren't always as they seem.

Around the time of my birth, my parents made a big move! They desired to "escape" the comfortable small town of Savannah, Georgia, and head for adventure in the state's capital city of Atlanta. Savannah was then, and to some degree still is, a BYOJ town: bring your own job.

In Atlanta, my dad landed his dream job. He was a Georgia Tech graduate and his new position allowed him to work in the Ford Motor Company assembly plant where they manufactured the snazzy Ford Torino. He loved it. He did not mind the long hours and night shift, which often ended in the wee hours of the morning. He thrived leading people and delighted in "playing" with cars. Mostly he relished driving home each night in a different sports car. Sometimes it was red, sometimes blue, sometimes black, but always fun.

Curiously, my mom, on the other hand, had a terrible time making friends. My siblings were ages two and five, and she carried me heavily in her belly. They spent the long, hot summer days playing in the front yard. Mom would grab a lawn chair, sit down, and snap a bucket of beans. She'd wave to the neighbors hoping to make a new friend. No one waved back or came by.

The next day she'd bring out some knitting and she'd place her chair further on the walkway to wave to the neighbors and no one would come by to welcome her to the neighborhood. This went on and on. Before long, she literally sat in the cul-de-sac, still without a friend.

Eventually she did make connections with these standoffish neighbors, and to this day, she enjoys close relationships with them. At some point she gathered the courage to say to them, "Why do you ignore me? Why do you not want to be my friend?"

They explained, "Honey, you have a baby in your belly. You have two young children. This is a wholesome family neighborhood. Yet, every night you're entertaining a new man. These men are always driving sports cars, sometimes red, sometimes blue...."

The power of perspective! It can truly be blinding. Life in my home was not as these neighbors assumed. In the same way, parenting can seem irrelevant to our careers. However, business is done with people, so people skills matter. *One effective way to build this acumen is to raise children.* Therefore, parenting matters, and parenting skills are indeed relevant to business success.

In her 2013 book *Lean In*, Sheryl Sandberg introduced the idea that our careers are more similar to jungle gyms of experience than linear paths up a corporate ladder. She does this for at least two reasons. First, Sandberg discourages us from scripting a specific limited path for our careers. As a speaker at the Stanford Graduate School of Business, she recently advised, "If you try to plan out your career, it's going to be boring. You're going to miss all the good stuff, because all the good stuff hasn't been invented yet."

The second reason she illustrates our careers as complex, varied jungle gyms is to encourage us to take *all* we learn on our lives' paths, to recall the "off-course" and sometimes untraditional know-how we have added to our toolbox and use their power to master the next opportunity.

In 2013, I had the pleasure of hearing Sheryl speak live at the Harvard Business School W50 conference, which was the fifty-year celebration of HBS accepting women. She is an alumnus of the school, and the timing of her book release afforded us this special opportunity. She concluded her inspiring remarks by requesting each woman in attendance

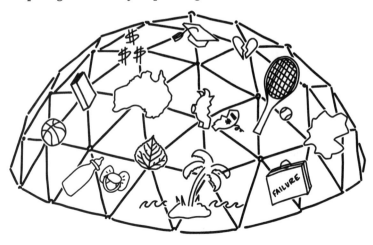

to rise to her feet and recognize her own personal accomplishments as well as the achievements of the other nine hundred women gathered in Burden Hall. With a regal wave and a stunning red dress, she exited the stage amidst the exuberant standing ovation.

I want you, too, to claim credit for all of your background. It breaks my heart to see people (very often women) belittling their experiences, relationships, and talents. Count them all, learn from them all, give yourself credit for them all, build on each one of them, and grow. *All* includes time away from the office while parenting. I submit that parenting is indeed a valid spot upon the career jungle gym.

Apparently, this already rings true for men but not for women. The *Wall Street Journal, New York Times, Business Insider*, and more have all written that women experience a "motherhood penalty," whereas men enjoy a "daddy bonus." Men who are fathers are paid more than men in similar positions who have no children. Conversely, women who are mothers are paid less than their childless counterparts.

In March 2018, Lydia DePillis of CNN reported, "There's a longstanding gap between the wages of mothers and those of childless women." She goes on to explain that this gap is 20 percent for mothers of three or more children.

The reasons behind the pay disparity are not clear. Neil Shah of the *Wall Street Journal* asserted:

> Much of this could also be outright discrimination: Some employers probably punish working mothers on the assumption that (a) they are the primary care-givers for children and (b) they will therefore have more unexpected mini-emergencies during the workday (having to suddenly pick up a sick kid). By this same logic, they may

reward fathers, thinking fathers will be more disciplined and focused—being fathers—and yet not have to actually fulfill as many parental duties. (Fathers, being more established in their careers, may also be more willing to demand raises.)

No wonder so many women treat parenting as a black smudge on their resume or LinkedIn profile, as if it is something to be covered up or hidden. Who would want a 20 percent pay decrease?

We are timid about displaying parenting as an asset on a resume because we don't fully recognize the value of parenting. I hope as I share some stories about my parenting lessons on collaboration, negotiation, communication, and more, you will also reflect on the expertise you gained (or are gaining) from parenting. I hope you talk about them, build on them, display confidence for having this savvy, and recognize similar prowess in your colleagues.

Together, we can not only bring more excellent ingenuity to the office, we can also get compensated fairly for doing so.

Imposter Syndrome

As we gather our gumption to face big decisions, choices, and goals, we need to address imposter syndrome. If you never experience it or don't know what I am talking about, then you might be an imposter reader of this book.... Naw, just kidding. If you don't know what I am talking about, I am truly thrilled. Hopefully that means you are not busily second-guessing yourself or doubting that you are sufficient for your current trial. Really. I pray that anyone within the grasp of this book sheds the habit of self-doubt immediately.

Harvard Business School addresses imposter syndrome right up front. Dean Kim Clark gathered all the entering class into Burden Hall—yes, I treasure that fifteen years later I sat in the same spot to hear Sheryl Sandberg. He didn't attempt to scare or intimidate us. He did not do the tough-guy act I have heard is so common at select schools. You know, the one that goes something like this: *turn to your right and to your left...those people will not be here when you graduate because x number of you will fail out*. Not at all. Dean Clark did the opposite. He said, "we don't make admissions mistakes. You are not an imposter of an HBS student. You are all meant to be here. You will be meeting amazing people this week, and it will be tempting to ask yourself, 'What am I doing here?' To think, 'I don't belong, I am an imposter.'" Rather, he instructed us to understand that each of us fit, and none of us were "imposters".

I now have a theory about imposter syndrome.

If you struggle with imposter syndrome, get really excited. It is evidence that you are taking tremendous action!

I spend a great deal of time with a wide variety of people. On the one hand, I am blessed to have a large group of friends that are almost exclusively from the same town where we live and they grew up. These people largely have maintained the same jobs or careers for decades and mostly spend their social time in the same circles. Although I enjoy their welcoming and warm friendship, I am not particularly inspired in their presence and I don't see them make a meaningful impact. Literally *none* of these mates are touched by imposter syndrome, and when I ask them about it, I am met with unregistering blank stares.

On the other hand, I have dozens of friends whose lives blow me away. I sit in awe of the uncertainty they embrace and the advancements they make. Many (not all) of these highly accomplished people are also incredibly well educated and have fancy pedigrees. Nevertheless, imposter syndrome is quite common amongst them.

In other words, in my personal experience, those who worry that they might be "imposters" are definitely *not*; conversely, those who don't recognize that they are imposters, to some degree, maybe are!

Please imagine a strong oak tree. My first friend group tends to reside solidly in the trunk of the tree where there is little change and tons of stability. They stay in the same jobs and live in the same town. I am not one of these people, but I am grateful to have them in my life. They provide a source of dependability, predictability, stability.

I don't gravitate to living in the tree's trunk or even on the branches. No, I tend to reside in the highest and farthest twig. Like a leaf, I reach to the sky and sway in the breeze. Unlike my stable buddies in the trunk, I am often plucked and sometimes crash to the ground only to rise again and grow.

What about you? My guess is that by the mere fact that you picked up this book—and made it through the first chapter embarking on new chances, challenges and changes—you might be more of a branch or leaf. Welcome! As the growing, stretching type, we will be prone to question ourselves. To see ourselves as imposters. Please waste no more energy questioning yourself. When that unease sneaks its pesky little way into your precious body, mind, or spirit, cringe your lip at it, grit your teeth if you have to, but then recognize it for what it is: confirmation that you are daring to live life out on the branches.

President Theodore Roosevelt famously said,

It is not the critic who counts; not the man who points out how the strong man stumbles, or where the doer of deeds could have done them better. The credit belongs to the man who is actually in the arena, whose face is marred by dust and sweat and blood; who strives valiantly; who errs, who comes short again and again, because there is no effort without error and shortcoming; but who does actually strive to do the deeds; who knows great enthusiasms, the great devotions; who spends himself in a worthy cause; who at the best knows in the end the triumph of high achievement, and who at the worst, if he fails, at least fails while daring greatly.

Things aren't always as they seem. Some days it will appear as though you are not fully equipped or qualified to handle the uncertainty and tests you face. But. You. Are! Just by jumping in the ring, you are winning!

On a practical note, time can also be deceiving. As parents, we learn that the days are long, but the years are short. I find that both professionally and personally, tasks that I expect will take fifteen minutes' worth of work turn out to be three hours! Does that happen to you? It is like the challenge is so clear in my head as I plan it that I assume it will roll out easily when it comes to execution. Alas, it does not.

My advice: Don't get frustrated. First, be sure to give yourself credit for the full three hours of what you have accomplished and *not* just the fifteen minutes. Once you get this job done, you won't have to do it again. Second, adjust your calendar and to-do list accordingly now that you know how long a certain sort of task will take. Set aside *right* amount of time—stop giving yourself fifteen minutes to handle three-hour tasks. You will just get started and then have to stop, then get frustrated. Finally, sometimes just opt out and *don't* do the task in front of you immediately.

One summer afternoon, when I was working many full-time jobs simultaneously, my dear friend Jen rang up to invite me and the kids to the pool. She also gave the option of her just taking my children so I could concentrate for an hour or so. I had a list of forty-six "to-dos." How could I go? I realized that I could stay home, miss out on a memory-making afternoon, and still have a list of forty-three to-dos remaining. This time I skipped work and enjoyed the moment.

Chapter 3

Embracing Failure, Failure Can Be Fabulous

"This isn't vacation, is it, Mom?" The question came from my fourteen-year-old daughter, who caught me hanging out laundry on a makeshift line in the vacation condo. At this moment, I learned exactly how the Grinch must have felt when Cindy Lou Who tiptoed in as he shoved the family Christmas tree up the chimney and her loving voice quietly asked, "Santie Claus, why? Why are you taking our Christmas tree? Why?" I was caught!

My innocent and loving daughter similarly wanted answers. How could I be truthful? We were broke. We were about to lose our beautiful home that we had custom built. We were supposed to grow old in the home and never leave. I had been so sure of that fact that in four rooms, I had hand painted tiles with the children, and those tiles were now set in the fireplace, showers in bathrooms, and the kitchen backsplash. The flower petals painted on the kitchen tiles were not random round dots, they were the thumb prints of the children. This was our home, our forever haven.

Yet I was months behind on mortgage payments, and at this point, I was staring down about $700,000 in personal debt from the real estate crash, mounting medical bills, and an unemployed spouse. Not ready to admit defeat, I devised a plan. The only thing I could think to do was to move out of our home for the summer and rent it out week by week to vacationers who were willing to pay a pretty penny to be on the Carolina coast. I planned excursions such that my sons experienced this summer as a glorious series of trips enjoying places like Uncle Bill's pool, Nana and Pop's beach town, and a friend's lake house. I carried my laptop with me, doing consulting work, and away we went. Each week I collected a big paycheck for the "vacation" rental that was our home currently stripped of family pictures and personal memorabilia. This particular week, we were just a block away from our home to check on things. In order to maximize the gap between income and expense for the week, I "rented" a nearly abandoned small condo that was riddled with problems, not the least of which was the broken clothes dryer. Thus, I was hanging our clothes on a line. My daughter had also noticed that the refrigerator was broken and currently held the milk jug in a scoop of melting ice. I was fooling nobody but myself.

No, it was not vacation. Like the Grinch, it was time for me to face reality. For ten years my marriage had been unraveling as debt and stress mounted. Divorce was imminent and my finances were a disaster. I failed big time! I failed my children, and I failed myself, by denying the storm headed our way.

What about you? I wonder if you picked up this book because you are recovering from a recent setback. Maybe you are ready to start thriving again. *I hope so.* You are at the right place. Perhaps, however, talking about messes is not your thing. Perhaps you are wondering why a book about business, learning, and parenting dedicates a whole chapter to failure. Maybe you are even skimming this chapter or sort of reading it sideways through one eye. I get it. I tried that trick when looking at my bank account. Sorry to inform you, but it never worked. The "reading through one eye closed" strategy doesn't change the reality of my bank statement, and it won't change any defeats you need to face head on. Flops are hard to admit, and we don't like to look at them. Nevertheless, we must. You have to. I have to. Let's do it together. What upsets haven't you faced? Look straight ahead and get going. I want to share about my mishaps big and small as a way of encouraging you to seek the same. Once we face them, we can accept and move on.

Some business schools "teach" disappointment by grading on a forced curve. For example, there are only three grade possibilities. The top 10% of each class receives a 1, the bottom 10% receives a 3, and the middle 80% receives a 2. There are many benefits to the system. Paramount is the introduction to defeat. Entrepreneurs and innovators know that misfiring is necessary for growth.

I once wrote, "Every entrepreneur has two master's degrees: one in success, one in failure." As an investor and advisor, I spent decades helping companies learn how to "fail fast." For us, that meant developing a skeleton of a product or service and acquiring loads of customer feedback early. I often encourage entrepreneurs to build only an MVP—minimally viable product—and not move a step further until they had met with one hundred prospects in order to understand their buying potential and feedback. If the product or service was going to fail, we wanted it to do so early on in the process.

Mothers also know intimately about imperfection...for our children and for ourselves. No human has popped out of the womb walking and talking. When I first started talking to women about this book, the moms who were entrepreneurs often said that motherhood prepared them for entrepreneurship because motherhood got them comfortable with inadequacy. Parenting is so much about trying, bungling, and trying again. It is about moving forward and not letting perfect be the enemy of the good. These women reported that parenting taught them it was okay to do the same in a professional front as well. So they were able to move quickly, grow often, and iterate and innovate in their business.

Yet I am worried. I see us raising a generation that has been denied the opportunity to fail. When I was a child, we allowed children to stumble, falter, and eventually grow up and earn victories through hard work. Today, youngsters seek glory, scoring, and recognition at insatiable rates, often leaving them frustrated and unfulfilled. Back in the day, we did not alter the sport to fit the child. However, today we have literally changed the way tennis, soccer, and basketball are played. I believe this has massive consequences socially, emotionally, and beyond.

I learned to play tennis in the fourth grade. None of us were coordinated enough to keep the very bouncy small yellow ball in play or to have a game that resembled a Chris Evert match. Instead we learned ball and racquet control. We were allowed to use the racquet to bounce the ball and keep it moving. As long as it didn't roll, we had endless opportunities to eventually get it over the net. As we progressed, we earned the right to play with fewer teammates to a side, later to compete limiting the number of bounces, and eventually to play with the real rules. Annually I watched Wimbledon on TV and recognized that I was personally getting closer to the real thing. I was working hard, and I was improving.

Today, everything is changed to fit the child and his or her ability...the ball is larger and squishy so it is easy to control. The score is kept just like it is on TV, and one implied message is "you are there...you are the same."

Similarly, when I played basketball as a young girl, I came home from games with a score of 2 to 4. One time it was only 2 to 0. The hoop was high and the ball heavy. But we kept trying. We learned to be determined. We missed and blundered and failed. It was exhilarating when the ball finally went in. We absolutely never even attempted a shot unless we were right under the basket. Why would we? Outside shots were for the college and NBA superstars and something we could grow into. Thus, we were subtly reminded that we were not the NBA where the scores were in the 80s and 90s.

Failure has immense power to motivate and instill patience. This is so critical that I want to also tap the wisdom of one of my heroes.

Brené Brown, author of *Daring Greatly*, talks about her best friend who teaches swimming and makes a principal observation about parenting today. The coach teaches a flip turn clinic and on that day requires each swimmer to do five proper flip turns before departing for the day. Each time the swimmer makes an attempt, the coach gives a hand signal: either two thumbs down for a failed attempt or two thumbs up for a successful flip turn. After a week of this, the coach received complaint letters and calls from the parents. "Could you please not do the thumbs down signal...maybe just one finger pointing to the side and not down?"

Brené illustrates how our unwillingness to allow negative feedback robs our children of those ecstatic moments when they reach success. Live it with me for a moment....

Flip turn attempt number one: nope.

Ugh, a thumbs down.

Flip turn attempt number two: nope.

Ugh, thumbs down again.

Flip turn attempt number three: nope.

Ugh thumbs down (frustration building but determination is too).

Flip turn attempt number 4: Yes! Success!

Two thumbs up! Big smile, victory...happiness!

Do you feel it? I do. It's exhilarating...motivating.

Perfect truly is the enemy of the good. It robs us and our youth today of learning, growing, connecting...we are all works in progress, and I hope we allow our classrooms, homes, and sports fields to be places of practice, not perfection.

What about at home? I am certain the cardinal thing I do as a mom is openly discuss my mistakes and apologize for them. Today's culture insists that everyone is a winner and must bring home a trophy. Yet, that hasn't been my personal experience, so I aim to be much more realistic with my children.

So far, my kids squirm a bit when I ask them to describe one of their weaknesses to me, and none of them jump into the dinner discussion with *let me tell you about today's debacle*. Yet, I am hopeful this taboo subject will evolve to mean opportunity, growth, and learning in such a way that risk taking is comfortable, not constricting.

A few years back, I had the dubious—yet delightful—position of leading an on-stage group discussion following Randi

Zuckerberg's speech during ImagiNATION 2013. It is not every day I meet a thirtysomething with a net worth exceeding $100 million. I knew she would be a hard act to follow, so I wanted to try something new and thought, "What would happen if we did introductions about our *defeats* and not our successes?"

Naturally, there was initially some skepticism with the other panelists, yet I pushed on, suggesting that my own introduction include facts like:

> "Bea attempted to lead an innovation center but was not selected for the final round of interviews. Bea played a significant role in launching four startup companies. One had a successful exit; the others suffered painful, long deaths. Bea received a 13 percent on her university biology dissection exam, flunked German class, and secured no roles through numerous musical auditions. We are delighted to welcome Bea Wray on Iterative Innovation and Cultural Challenges."

Soon, the other panelists were eager to also illustrate "ice-breaking" yet inviting visions of comeback as they crafted their own "bomb" introductions.

Allow me to share the great victory story which was born from one of the missteps I just mentioned. When I attended HBS, each student was permitted to take a language class for free at Harvard College, across the Charles River. I like to get my money's worth and tuition *is* very expensive. Additionally, I thought it would be exciting to walk through the iconic quadrangle, and I didn't want to miss the chance to enroll in a course amidst that historic environment. I decided to sign up for German. I rode my bike across the Charles River every day and attended German I. At first, these whippersnapper undergraduates were like, "Whoa, a business school student. She'll be intimidating." (Yes, I actually overheard that conversation.) Well, they had all taken German four or even five years in high school, and they were just in German I for their easy A. I, on the other hand, was truly looking for an introduction to the language. Eventually, the professor came to me, patted me on the shoulder, and said, "Even if you get a 100 on the exam, you will flunk the course. Please don't bother coming to the exam."

Dang!

Crestfallen, but determined, I ran home, stomped my foot, and said, "Guess what, we're moving to Germany! By God, if Harvard can't teach me German, the Germans will have to!"

My then-husband was brilliant at speaking German and was the reason I chose that language over the other options. He handled the conversation well, saying, "If you get a job there, we can go." It was 1999, the height of the Internet boom, I was in high tech and graduating from a prestigious school near the top of my class. I received three job offers. So we moved. For me, getting to Europe was the result of a botched attempt. Living in Europe as a young professional couple was one of the best experiences of my life.

I did learn one salient thing in German class. On page 491 of our textbook, a call-out box explained that women received six months maternity leave in Germany. I worked for Siemens, and we had a precious baby girl within a year. And I learned enough German to get around, sing "Backe, Backe Kuchen" to my children, and later volunteer as an elementary school German teacher. Professionally and personally, this fiasco emerged into one of my greatest life "wins!"

So, what about you? Is there any place where Cindy Lou Who might be asking you to take a hard look in the mirror? Are you ready to face your own deficits? Can you give yourself a "thumbs down" on a few items? If so, you are in good company *and* we are ready to move on to the meat of this book's journey—where we really begin to grow!

Part 2

Primary Success Skills

- Your Attitude Determines Your Altitude:
The Power of Staying Positive

- Going for Great with Gratitude

- Resilience, Grit, Tenacity:
Whatever You Call It, You're Gonna Need It!

- Communication Can Be Complex

- They May Not Remember What You Said,
But They'll Never Forget That You Listened

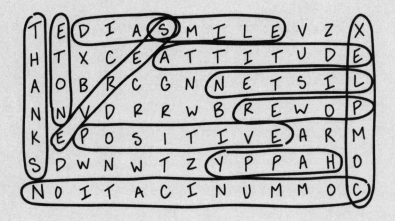

Chapter 4

Your Attitude Determines Your Altitude

THE POWER OF STAYING POSITIVE

"I don't understand how you do everything that you do"
is a comment I often heard when I was the sole caretaker and provider for three young children while working
multiple full-time jobs. The question was inevitably followed
by "and how do you do it with a smile?"

"Because it would be impossible to do it with a frown!"
was my truthful reply. Think about it; if you have to run a race,
you want the ability to use both legs. You don't want to hop on
one foot. Yet, when it comes to making the most of every day,
we can unwittingly slip into self-sabotage. When we show up
with less than a stellar perspective, we show up with one hand
behind our back for the most important game: *life*.

During the most trying days of my failed marriage, I didn't want crying to catch me off-guard, so I scheduled it for 5:00 a.m. each morning. My iTunes play count reveals the same song was used 137 times to allow me to weep out my hurts each morning before I faced my children with a smile. I listened to Éponine from *Les Misérables* sing "I Dreamed a Dream" to accompany my feelings. I truly felt "life had killed my dream." I cried until seven. By then I was ready to greet my children with a cheerful smile, which often was the most important accomplishment of the day.

Our culture of negativity is indeed an epidemic that needs healing. In this chapter, we will learn what is harmful about living with bad moods, and how we allow adversity to infiltrate our thinking. Additionally, we will see compelling evidence that choosing a great mindset creates success in every area of our lives.

A wonderful demeanor breeds energy, connection, and creativity.

To begin, let's recognize that life is not always easy, and situations are not always good. I find both in my work and my family, I need to create room for constructive feedback and comments. The best business schools institute feedback loops such as direct comments, mid-course surveys, and end-of-the-term student evaluations. These tools allow professors to gain knowledge. They also clear the air when problems pop up and create space for open participation. Similarly, in a work environment, the feedback loop could be 360-degree evaluations where annual performance conversations take place with bosses, peers, and direct reports.

"There are just too many hours in the day! I have nothing but time!" said no working parent ever. Right? Knowing how prone we are to feeling overwhelmed, overworked, and stressed, why would we not embrace the one easy-access tool which will stretch each hour and minimize our stress? Yes, a great temperament will literally increase your energy. I remember as a college student waiting tables at the Hofbräuhaus restaurant. Something sad, frustrating, or demanding with schoolwork or friends would happen in the afternoon, causing me to want to react in a gloomy way. Fortunately, my superior, Susan, was a career professional who insisted I put on a smile whether I felt like it and meant it or not. Within an hour or two, I actually felt much better and happier. Is that because I was smiling? Is that because people started to smile back at me? I think yes and yes. At times we must act ourselves into right thinking!

We want to spiral upward, not downward. The first step is to recognize that we have a choice: our behavior can direct our feelings. We do not need to let awful feelings direct our behavior. Connecting with others is my personal favorite benefit of selecting a pleasing reaction. I only smiled a few times in the restaurant before I felt the glow of the smiles of my customers and coworkers.

On the other hand, a poor bent often serves as a repellent to the very people we need to captivate. Training your team to practice affirmation is essential to improving your business results. Lately, it seems when I am a customer at a retail or food and beverage establishment, I am met with negativity. "I get off in an hour!" or "My shift is almost done!" may be true statements; however, they are not helpful. They tend to make the customer feel unwelcome, and they deplete energy. We can train ourselves and our teams to speak uplifting narratives like, "I am happy I am able to serve you today!"

Creativity is birthed through positive energy. I have a stunning picture of my teenage ballerina daughter doing a scorpion at sunrise. A scorpion is an actual dance move where the dancer stands on the toes of her foot while the toes of the other foot are clasped in hands above and beyond her head. The body and arched back with arms along with the extended leg form a circle which appears to sit upon the pedestal of the leg upon which she is standing. This move is beautiful and difficult. It requires strength, balance, and flexibility. In the picture, through the circle that Savannah's body creates, the sun is rising, the timing is perfect, and the image is breathtaking. A friend saw the picture, and I have never forgotten his reaction: "Wow! In an age of depressed anxious teenagers, look at that creativity and stellar attitude!" He saw it for what it was, artistic expression which can only emerge from a mindset of abundance, not scarcity. His observation taught me that choosing a great mental state is not just a tool for combatting what is bad. More importantly, embracing a "can-do" spirit is foundational for breaking the chains of self-limitations and originating what is good.

Choose language wisely, both narrative and lexicon. Our tongues are the most powerful muscles in our bodies, so we need to select carefully what we say to others and even more importantly to ourselves. When I talk about narrative, I am referring to the story I tell myself. I am not abdicating lying, but rather being intentional about repeating the most empowering stories. When I am launching a company, should I recount to myself about all the companies that fail? How many people much smarter than me have had to close their doors? How other people obtained financing, but I did not? Maybe, where there are lessons to learn. It is the ceaseless fretting that must end.

It is more invigorating to tell myself a different narrative. The focus could be the handful of prospective clients with whom I have an excellent relationship. I can list the contacts who have told me they have a need for my services and desire to work with me.

Word choice matters, and we can construe our own lexicon. One of my dearest friends, Janette, transitioned her career from speech pathologist to executive coach. Just that transition alone epitomizes the magnitude speech has on the ability to coach. Each conversation with her is uplifting largely because of the language she chooses. She encourages me to ask myself questions like, "What do I love in my life right now?"

Additionally, Janette pushes me to rephrase "I can't..." into "up until now, I have not been successful at...." Finally, her advice is always delivered with a gentle nudge: "I invite you to consider...." Janette never delivers suggestions with "you should" or "you need." By contrast, another buddy smothers me with so much "you need" that I started to tease that "Eunide" must be her best pal.

Do you have a to-do list? If it works for you, keep it up. I, however, do not like knowing that there is an endless list of things that need to get done. The reminder hanging over my head can slow me down rather than speed me up. I do like tricks that help me remember things, like I might set aside specific time to reply to certain emails or to properly file important forms. But lists can intimidate and overwhelm me, zapping my energy. I find it more motivating to create a "have done" list with all my accomplished tasks of the day.

The scarcity/abundance meter is a mini exercise for turning up the dial on your creative energy through narrative and lexicon. Do you think about what you have (time, talents, resources, connections, and so on) and decide that you are lacking (in other words, there is a scarcity)? Or, do you take inventory and recognize you have all you need to take the next step (in other words, there is an abundance)? Try it, please. Wherever you find yourself on the theoretical scarcity/abundance meter, make an effort to take a step or two towards abundant thinking.

The best volunteer coordinators do not bemoan the fact that they are understaffed. Rather, they praise the existing volunteers, the impact they are making, and the fulfillment they are experiencing. "Mmmm, yummy," says every great mother in front of her children while eating broccoli. You get the idea. Imagine a magnet, not a rake.

Finally, perspective matters. I once attended a seminar with Seth Goldman, the founder of Honest Tea. He is a very well-educated, successful, and wealthy man. So it was refreshing to learn from his simple approach. Seth stood up and, with a marker, wrote on the flipchart: Have > Want = Happiness. He went on to explain that for all of us, if we have more than we want, we will find happiness. So, most of us work and work to *have more*. However, Seth explained that a more expedient path to happiness is to decide to *want less*.

In his top-ten TED Talk "The Happy Secret to Better Work," Shawn Achor explains "What we're finding is it's not necessarily the reality that shapes us, but the lens through which your brain views the world that shapes your reality." Stay tuned for more from Shawn—he is the star of chapter 16: Write Your Own Ticket!

In summary, cultivating a winning approach is a choice, requires an affirmative narrative and vocabulary, and is shaped by our choice of perspective. Finally, adding positivity also requires letting go of negativity.

Three areas I want to explore to help us let go of negativity include the victim mentality, twenty-four-hour media, and the culture of "busy."

Someone stole $60 from me, so I threw away $86,340. That's right. It is not a typo. Someone stole $60 from me, so I threw away $86,340. I believe if you think about it, you will find you have done the same thing. My point assumes time is money. If every second is a dollar, this conversion is exact. Even if it is not, the lesson is valuable. I am guilty. Too often when someone has been antagonistic to me, or even just crummy around me, for 60 seconds, I have thrown away the rest of my day (86,340 remaining seconds) by allowing the lousy energy to consume me and my thoughts, zapping productivity and creativity. Sometimes I throw away the whole week...you do the math.

What about you?

Now, I ask you, if you had $86,400 and someone stole $60, would you throw away the $86,340 for revenge? Or move on and live? The best retaliation for any attack is to propel forward and live a fulfilling life.

Each of us have 86,400 seconds every day. Don't let someone's bitter 60 seconds ruin the remaining 86,340. In my calculation, I included sleep time in the full twenty-four hours, because I am embarrassed to admit that I have sometimes allowed acrimony to also impact my sleep.

I am *not* suggesting that we should be doormats. Whenever we have been mistreated, we should stand up for ourselves appropriately to the people or person who can correct the problem. Better yet, command respect from the start! What I am trying to convey is the huge burden and cost we place on ourselves in reaction to a wrongdoing when we choose to extend the pain by playing the victim. Often when a relationship sours, there are two distinct parts. Consider a circle cut into two equal parts. On the left side there are unmet expectations, broken promises, and the like. On the right side we find sadness, disappointment, frustration, and so on. I will give you the left. Those are things we cannot change, and I am truly heartbroken that they happen to you. But the right is there waiting for you. Claim it back. *Now.*

As a business motivational speaker primarily to audiences of women, I have plenty of opportunities to address inequalities women face. The first thing I encourage women to do is to assume that the workplace is fair, and the best jobs and best pay are given to those that take risks, raise their hands, and speak up. A great pet peeve of mine is a speaker talking to all women about those "bad white men who treat us poorly." If they are not in the room, then talking about it only zaps the empowerment from those very capable people who *are* there. I don't actually believe that all things are fair. Nevertheless, we have an opportunity to reject the victim mentality that renders us powerless so that we can take meaningful, actionable steps towards a more just society.

Secondly, we relinquish negativity when we recognize how media breeds hostility. Ted Turner founded twenty-four-hour media through CNN in 1979. I believe he truly thought we would all benefit from learning about important worldwide developments with a chance to expand our minds beyond our immediate surroundings. Unfortunately, the unintended consequence has been the opposite. Today, we tend to get one hot story and obsess over that story for hours and days straight. The news becomes repetitive, inflammatory, and very opinionated.

America's most trusted man, Walter Cronkite, instilled a calm through the sixties and seventies, signing off the nightly news with "that's the way it is." In contrast, today's news is designed to keep us agitated and tuned in with each broadcaster literally saying, "don't go away" or "stay right here!" Amazingly, like dogs wearing a shock collar, we do it! How productive is that?

My first child was born in October of 2000. We lived in Munich, Germany, and I felt a little homesick. So, when I got up in the middle of the night to nurse her, I would turn on the American news just to hear English being spoken and feel closer to home. This was a bad idea, as it was during the recount of the Gore vs. Bush Presidential election. Greta Van Susteren's voice was agitated as she dramatized hanging chads. Just hearing her strain made me tense. I eventually realized that even the baby could sense the stress, and that played a major role in her becoming colicky. With hindsight, it seems so obvious to me now that my state of mind would impact the mood of my baby. Yet these things are studied and "proven" scientifically, so perhaps I was not the only person who didn't see the connection as obvious. The *Journal of Experimental Psychology* summarizes, "results suggest that mothers' affective states—low-arousal positive states as well as high-arousal negative states—can be "caught" by their infants, and that touch can play a critical role in stress contagion."[1]

Not only was I initially not observant about how my daughter was feeding off my mood, I was naive to how I was feeding off the mood of the TV reporter. Today when I Google

---

1   Waters, S. F., West, T. V., Karnilowicz, H. R., & Mendes, W. B. (2017). "Affect contagion between mothers and infants: Examining valence and touch." *Journal of Experimental Psychology*: General, 146(7), 1043–1051. https://doi.org/10.1037/xge0000322)

"media induced anxiety," forty-three scholarly articles result. Indeed, we must be diligent in our efforts to not let constant news bring us down.

Finally, as we shed inferior inclinations, let's address the culture of busyness. Today, I'm listening to the rain. Yesterday, I watched the leaves blow in the wind. The next time someone asks you, "What are you doing?" I dare you to answer some descriptive enjoyment of nature or reply simply, "relaxing." Too often our answer is a litany of duties. I enjoyed impeccably manicured lawns and blooming flowers daily in the non-snow months. This taught me an intentional appreciation of the outdoors. Similarly, if my children have made me learn anything, it is to truly embrace the moment and feel dread subside as I do.

I will close the chapter on having an excellent mental posture by sharing three tools: service, margin, and gratitude. Regular community service is the best antidote to shoddy energy. My business school knows this and thus offers endless clubs with connections to local schools and nonprofits. When my son was struggling with aggression, serving at the local food bank had a much greater impact than discipline or discussion.

Margin is simply the idea of building a cushion. Arrive early. Drive the speed limit. Give yourself the gift of blocked time on your calendar for meeting preparation as well as follow up. I used to believe that I didn't have time to do any of these things. I now know I don't have time not to do them. All of chapter 12 is dedicated to building margin through efficiency tools.

Practicing gratitude is the most important tool for sustaining an exceptional character. Thus, it deserves its own chapter. Thanks for staying positive, soaring at high altitudes, and meeting me in chapter 5!

Photo by Bea Wray

Chapter 5

Going for Great
with Gratitude

"Robert Wray! Robert Wray! You know Robert Wray?" My fourteen-year-old daughter invited me to go to a Halloween party with a group of parents while she and her friends went trick-or-treating in the neighborhood. Only a few of us adults knew each other, so we gathered over appetizers to get acquainted.

A woman asked whose mom I was. "My daughter Savannah is out with the girls," I said. "I also have two sons: Robert Wray, and his younger brother—"

I never finished my sentence. A man who heard me on the other side of the room came over and said, "Robert Wray! You know Robert Wray?"

And then he pulled out his phone and started swiping through dozens of photos.

My heart sank.

Uh-oh. What did Robert do? Is he in trouble? Am I in trouble?

Finally, the man stopped swiping, held up his phone, and showed me the image he'd been looking for—a note from Robert thanking him for his leadership and encouragement during a summer sports camp.

I smiled, and I could feel my heart swell.

"This is why we do what we do," the man claimed. "I carry Robert's note with me everywhere. I even shared it with my entire team. I went to the mailbox that day hoping there'd be a check inside, because we were down on funding.

"That was all I wanted—a check. But when I read Robert's note, I knew it was better than any check."

I'd never seen that letter before; I didn't even know Robert had sent it. But it was super sweet.

Now my heart soared because this man I was speaking with was not the only one who benefited from my son's act of gratitude. He shared the letter with his team members, and it lifted their spirits, too.

That's how gratitude works. Telling someone you're grateful creates a far-reaching ripple effect. Done well, it ignites a flow of energy that can't be contained.

It has a greater impact on the giver than on the receiver. When I'm worn out, I make a list of things I'm grateful for, and it feeds me. Showing gratitude is empowering.

I'm a longtime fan of thank-you notes. In fact, I believe my commitment to writing them was a major reason I was accepted to Harvard Business School.

There were nine essay questions on my application form, and one of them stood out: *Describe a typical day.*

I don't remember my exact words, but I wrote that my typical workday began with a morning run at the base of the Golden Gate Bridge and ended with writing thank-you notes.

I spent the last ten to fifteen minutes of every day reviewing the appointments on my calendar and hand-writing quick thank-you notes to each person I'd met.

My essay explained that this was my reflection time—my chance to relax and fill myself with the energy that is literally manufactured from displaying gratitude. I couldn't help but recognize the blessing of having people interested in our growing business. And in that frame of mind, I never felt overwhelmed by the worries that consume many salespeople and early-stage entrepreneurs. While others were fretting about making their monthly numbers, my mind was filled with creative energy that would fuel my vision and passion for weeks.

In today's fast-paced culture, very few of us write thank-you notes. But I'm convinced we should, because when we take time to acknowledge others, we stand out from the crowd.

I know this because it worked for me. When I would call to follow up on proposals and potential partnerships, I almost always got a warm reception, one that was very different from the stiff arm most salespeople know too well.

Many of my sales relationships lasted for years. And in some cases, decades.

I met Diana, one of my dearest friends, more than twenty-five years ago at computer law conferences. I lived in San Francisco at the time, and she was in Chicago, but the more than two thousand miles between us did not stop us from building a relationship.

Attendees at many of the law conferences we went to marginalized me as "just a vendor." Yet Diana wanted to invest in a business relationship with me—mainly because of the brief notes I wrote to her after every gathering.

Today, after dozens of transitions, Diana and I continue to share the joys and heartaches of our lives. We even ended up as carpool buddies for one special stretch. Investing in this relationship has paid huge dividends for both of us, and gratitude was our starting point.

It's why I've tried to make it a vital element of every position I've held since.

I once served as the executive director of The Creative Coast in Savannah, Georgia, and we wrote plenty of thank you-notes—because raising funds was essential, as it is at all non-profits.

We had hundreds of donors and partners whose gifts covered our operational funding, events, and programming, and we made it our business to write a thank-you note to every one of them.

Interestingly, nearly every day, someone also said thank you to me. We served hundreds of people through mentorships, business plan competitions, innovation conferences, and an entrepreneur incubator, and people would come along and say thank you—even with a handwritten note now and then.

I vividly recall one day when there were dozens of thank-you notes we'd received at one end of a table, waiting for me to read them, and there was a stack of thank-you notes our team had written—sealed, addressed, stamped, and ready to be mailed—on the other end.

This was an indelible image.

When I went home that night, I was feeling overwhelmed by my work and family responsibilities. I had three children—a first-grader, a kindergartener, and a toddler—and the sun was setting when I looked up from my last emails of the day.

I was trying to figure out how to get everything done. I had to make dinner, feed the baby, give everyone a bath, and help with homework.

My daughter's assignment was to read for fifteen minutes, my son's was to have someone read to him for fifteen minutes, and in my desperate state I fretted, "Where will I get those thirty minutes?"

And then it hit me—my daughter could read to my son.

Done and done! I relaxed, had a glass of wine, and enjoyed the rest of my evening.

The next day, back at the office, I took another glance at those two stacks of note cards and had an *aha!* moment....

Why is my team writing notes to our funders and getting notes from the people we serve? Wouldn't it be smarter to let the funders hear directly from the people who benefit from their generosity?

So we changed our process. We kept the dozens of envelopes we'd already addressed and stamped for our donors, but we kept the cards blank. And when an entrepreneur or student came in for consulting, or an event, or a podcast recording, or any sort of assistance, I would ask, "Did you have a good experience? What was good about it?"

In most cases, they would rave about how much they appreciated what we'd done for them. And then I'd ask:

"Before you leave, would you kindly consider writing your thoughts in a note to one of our funders? Just write the things you received from us that you're grateful for—but, please, don't write it to me. Write it directly to the people who write the checks that make our work possible."

And just about all of them said they'd be delighted to stick around for five more minutes and write a quick note that said something like, "I came to The Creative Coast, and they helped me hone my business plan. I'm so grateful that you support this organization...."

As a bonus, many of them were college students, and they loved the opportunity to connect with some of the most powerful people in town. We encouraged them to include their own business card in with their thank-you note.

Everybody won. The young entrepreneurs and students were developing a critical skill, our funders loved hearing directly from them that their money was making an impact, and—maybe best of all—my overstretched staff had one less task to do.

Flushed with success at work, I decided to get systematic about gratitude when I got home. This meant two things:

First, all of us would have a journal in which we'd list ten things every day for which we were grateful.

Second, all of us would write one thank-you note each day.

I began to buy thank-you cards in batches of three hundred, and I discovered something amazing and heartwarming:

I used to come home exhausted after a long day of work and my one-hour commute, and I could get frustrated and downright grumpy if my family met me at the door with a barrage of questions about what I was going to make for dinner, or could I take them out shopping.

But when my kids wrote a thank-you note every day, they were more likely to meet me at the door with, "Hi, mom! How was your day? I love you!"

And that changed everything. It set the tone for a wonderful evening.

When we started writing our daily thank-you notes, I asked the kids to pick a teacher, or a coach, or a neighbor, or a grandparent to appreciate. The boys were so young that their notes were often more like drawings than writing. My job was to track down the addresses, put stamps on the envelopes, and get them in the mail.

But sometimes I dropped the ball, and then a month or two later, one of my children would find a thank-you note they'd written tucked in a stack of incoming mail or school flyers. Now I was in trouble.

On a few occasions, I came across a written note with a name on the envelope, but no address or stamp—and I didn't have a clue when it was written or what it was about. Sometimes I got lucky. If the note were written to a close friend who knew how disorganized I could be, I'd think, *Yay, look what I found!* and I'd scribble "Better Late Than Never!" on the coffee-stained envelope, pop it in the mail, and wait to laugh with them when they told me their story of opening it.

But I have to confess; knowing the recipient of the note felt appreciated was only half the benefit for me. The other half was the palpable knowledge that writing those notes was shaping the hearts of my children.

I understood their frustration when I failed to get those notes into the mail. I knew I couldn't keep them motivated if I didn't do a better job. So I stepped up my game.

I proactively addressed and stamped dozens of envelopes to be sent to extended family members, teachers, and other important people. These sat in a basket in the kitchen so that a child could select one each day. Once the cards were written, they were ready to go.

It was a good system, and it worked for a while—but eventually, life got in the way, we got a bit lazy, and stopped doing the daily notes.

Months later, when we were moving to a new home, I came across some envelopes. They were fully addressed and stamped and even appeared to be sealed (with hindsight I realize they were only half-sealed because we live in the moist climate of the South). I temporarily forgot about my blank-card-ready system and thought, *Oh no, these are cards that never made it to the mailbox!*

I grabbed three of them—one for my niece and two for nephews—and popped them in the mail. *Better late than never!*

And that, my friends, is how my niece and two nephews got blank cards in the mail.

In fact, one nephew got the card on his birthday! We have a picture of him holding it up with a big smile. When his brilliant mom saw the blank note, she immediately invented the concept of invisible ink. *Imagine what it says*, she told the birthday boy.

I don't feel the urge to provide tips and tricks for doing gratitude "right." There truly is no wrong. All I can say is, become aware of how you show gratitude. Whether you write thank-you notes, make lists, set aside gratitude minutes... that's up to you. Just do it.

My desire is to tell you how grateful I am that you're reading this book. You encourage me. You inspire me. You guide me. You provide clarity to my thinking and meaning to my madness.

So I say this sincerely, from the bottom of my heart:
Thank you.

Chapter 6

Resilience, Grit, Tenacity
WHATEVER YOU CALL IT, YOU'RE GONNA NEED IT!

Have you ever struggled to put a toddler to bed? Did you lose the battle? Yeah, I know how you feel. Hopefully this chapter will be encouraging to you. Some of that toddler's determination is exactly what we as parents strive to nurture in our children.

Grit, tenacity, resilience, determination, stubbornness, doggedness—whatever you call it, I have it to a fault. I am the one person I know who has been down in a tennis match 6–0, 5–0 and has come back to win. I wish I could tell you I did so because I had hope, I knew I could do it, or I saw victory in the middle of defeat. That wasn't it.

I was playing in a real tournament for the first time when I was about twelve years old. I loved tennis (still do) and had been playing for a while but had never actually registered as a competitor and shown up to play in a tournament. My dad thought it would be a good experience. My mom was befuddled by the ten-dollar registration fee: "Why does it cost ten dollars when the balls, a T-shirt, and the court time are not even included? What does the ten dollars cover?"

Of course, I laugh now, as I know people who have spent $32,000 a year on their children achieving USTA rankings, traveling to God knows how many cities for sanctioned tournaments, and enrollment into elite tennis academies. But for us, at that time, ten dollars was the family conversation, and quite frankly, it was getting on my nerves. I was excited to compete in my first tournament. Initially, to be a part of the hustle and bustle of dozens of girls heading out to ten different courts *was* exciting. Yet, the ten dollars dominated my thoughts. In my match, I found myself down 6–0, 5–0. Ugh. How could I go home now? I just had to stretch out the match. So, I tried to make each point last longer, just keeping the ball in play. I never once thought, "I can win this thing." I didn't look that far into the future. I simply wanted to stay on the court. All the courts around us finished and the girls went home. Later, the tournament organizer went home. The lights came on. We kept playing. I continued getting one more shot back. I became so tired, I relied on my opponent to keep the score. We went to a third set. Eventually she was so tired, she looked at our dads to tell her the score. I kept hitting one more shot. The match was a fight to the end, and somehow, as we completed the final point and jogged to the net to shake hands, I was the winner.

At that stage, I didn't care that much about the match victory as I knew I had uncovered something deep inside me that I would never lose. I learned that I didn't know how to give up.

Many moons later, my sister-in-law said the same thing referring to my marriage with her brother, "You don't know how to admit defeat." She was not just a bonus sibling that comes with the package of matrimony. We had become such dear friends that I even had the privilege of being the matron of honor in her own wedding. She cared almost as much about my marriage as I did. Nevertheless, it had failed, miserably, repeatedly.

I went back to my broken marriage four different times. New Year's Eve in 2009, I made one more major internal commitment that we *were* going to make it work. I committed to give everything I could in the year 2010 to save our marriage. I changed all the passwords on bank accounts, email addresses, and so on to "StayMarried10." Over the next few years, my children were approaching their teens and were always helping me with this or that, especially when it came to technology and passwords. Unfortunately though, things within my marriage continued to spiral out of control. Imagine my wake-up call when one of my children said, "Hey mom, can we switch the password to 'GetDivorced14'?"

Although my stick-to-it-iveness is not always convenient, it was handy during that tennis match. In fact, I've learned that often our worst qualities are tied to our best. For me, persistence is the single factor for any success I have personally enjoyed in my career.

I started my company, SourceHarbor, in 2003. At that time, we had only $4,000 worth of revenue and were being sued by a $1.8 billion company. The company leaders spent $500,000 suing us because we "were putting them out of business." Talk about a bad day!

Two days earlier, my family and I had arrived in San Francisco for a nine-week stay. It had been hectic getting out there, so I was looking forward to settling in. Then I was pumped to focus on establishing our West Coast office. I didn't like traveling away from my family for business when my children were small, so I found ways to bring them with me (more about that in chapter 13). One evening, my husband grilled dinner outside as I nursed my six-month-old and my two-year-old daughter played with toys at my feet. Suddenly, the doorbell rang, and I answered with baby in tow. Shockingly, I was served a two-inch-thick stack of legal papers regarding a very aggressive predatory lawsuit.

By the end of the week, my legal bill was over $25,000. I called my investors back east and let them know what was happening. Immediately, they all told me to give up and to tend to my family. They did not care about their financial loss, as their investments had been small. They knew we had done nothing wrong. The more supportive they were and the more they cared more about me as a person, the more I wanted to fight to save the company and the less I wanted to throw in the towel.

Three months later, the lawsuit still consumed us and finally settled, leaving me with a $384,000 legal bill. Remember, at that time our company had only $4,000 of revenue!

We didn't have the resources to continue the fight all the way until we won back legal fees and damages. However, in a sense we did *win* because we survived. The real victory was that we went on to build SourceHarbor into a company that served thousands of clients across fourteen countries. When I finally sold it years later, it was the best performer in my key investor's portfolio.

In sum: grit, tenacity, perseverance, resilience, and success all come from the desire and ability to stay the course.

Harvard has published numerous cases on organization as well as personal grit and stamina. They also practice what they preach. They know the emotional, social, and financial value of alumni. When I was devastated financially and embarrassed to reach out to my network, they wouldn't let me go. For that tenacity I am grateful.

For the sake of expanding our skills, let's think of grit as the individual grit that keeps us going and resilience as "group grit," if you will. Resilience is the strength that brings us together and makes us powerful as one body. I was invited to host a TEDx event as the emcee. The TEDx event took place on Hilton Head Island along the South Carolina coast not long after Hurricane Matthew. The organizers chose "Resilience" as the theme since the island had been hit hard by the storm yet rallied together for a remarkable comeback. After the mandatory one-week evacuation, Byron Sewell spray-painted a plywood sign (pictured below) to welcome residents home. This spark brought individuals together.

As the emcee, I contemplated this powerful story and the meaning of the word *resilience*. I saw RE-SILIENCE. I realized that inside the word *resilience* is *silence*. And what I realized is the way to be vulnerable or the opposite of resilient is to stay silent, to not raise your hand, to be alone. So the solution is to insert myself (the word *I*) into silence, in order to interrupt the silence. I insert myself by reaching out, by making a phone call, by creating a friend, by serving. Then the most important part of the word *resilience* is the prefix *re*, meaning "again and again." Resilient communities are built when members interrupt the silence again and again.

Amazingly, as I write this chapter, my community, state, country, and world are all on lockdown. It is the coronavirus pandemic. There are constant emails, news broadcasts, and social media posts about the importance of staying connected. We universally understand that there is safety in numbers. It is no wonder Zoom Video Communications stock price is soaring.

Photo by Amy Glos

Remember that toddler? My daughter did not sleep through the night for her first fourteen months. They say the definition of colic is crying inconsolably for three hours or more a day for six days a week. Well, she cried closer to six hours a day, which meant that I cried for three! So, there I was, a thirty-two-year-old with colic. At one point when she should have had two naps and one sleep a day, I was basically rocking and consoling her for two hours three times a day.

I remember arguing with her, "This is not what I had planned as a mother! We are supposed to be at the park, feeding ducks, smelling flowers...." I was *so* frustrated. Well, if you had told me then that those tough fourteen months would feed into a practically perfect next fourteen-plus years, I would not have complained. Lucky me, she's never given me a minute of trouble since.

Savannah was so determined to succeed in school and attend a small liberal arts school that she only befriended the smartest kid in her grade. When that person changed schools or moved away or got distracted by social temptations, Savannah "best friended" the next smartest kid. Her grit carried me and my sons through years that should have been filled with turmoil. Today, she is thriving at Vassar College.

Visually, we were able to enjoy the beauty of her stick-to-it-ness one memorable evening. In the seventh grade, Savannah was selected as the role of Marie in *The Nutcracker*. This was my favorite season of the year as we knew most of the families of the fifty ballerinas who performed throughout the six shows. It served as a recital in some ways for dozens of young girls. Additionally, it was an incredible production which brought in a few professional ballet dancers from classical ballet companies around the country for premier and partnering roles. On this particular Friday evening, the theater was packed, yet there was a problem. The production manager had spent the day in the hospital, and no one else was trained in his responsibilities, such as opening and closing curtains, dimming and brightening lights, and ensuring the correct music is played and well timed. "Should we cancel the show?" everyone wondered, but it was decided the show must go on!

When it came time for Savannah's solo, she was ready and poised. She had rehearsed for five hours a day for months. The music started but it was the wrong music. The last-minute fill-in person had made a mistake. Savannah danced. Her leaps were flawless, her smile was electrifying, her performance was stunning. Savannah's solo morphed into a dance where fifteen other party girls were to follow her lead. They did. It was seamless even though it began with the wrong music. Most of the six hundred people in the audience never noticed any problem. I, however, will never forget when the dancer from the Houston Ballet said to me after the show that he had never seen anything like it. Most people would have gotten frustrated, stalled, waited for the music to get changed, and in doing so would have brought all the attention to the problem. Not Savannah. The same baby who refused to go to sleep at naptime became the girl who refused to let anything get in the way of her special moment.

What about my tennis opponent? She is a superstar who went on to become the captain of her Ivy League tennis team and is now an executive at the Tennis Channel. Many years after our first encounter, I ran into her and she graciously credited our match as playing a role in her success. Which leads me to an exercise I want you to do. Have you ever been defeated, rejected, cut from a team, or denied acceptance to a fellowship, university, or the like? Please write that person or institution a letter and begin with "Thank you for being a part of my grit story." Continue to admire their work or whatever it was about them that made you want to apply in the first place, wish them well, and share the hope your paths will again someday cross. Then dig deep and commit to improving, growing, and living your best life.

Both grit and resilience are important in sales. Through tenacity and time, relationships are cultivated, and business can grow through the trust that is formed. Call after call, follow-up after follow-up, sales grit produces results.

Resilience is also relevant to business growth. Apparently, I made one memorable comment in marketing class. It was that excellent sales are more like a zipper than a snap. My advice is that companies should not aim to have one point of contact offer their services to one point of contact at the prospect's organization. Rather, the relationship should be fortified more like a zipper with multiple connections throughout the company including the department needing the service, senior leadership, purchasing, and so on. Each one should have a correlating attentive representative helping to make an effective and profitable sale. Back for my fifth reunion, my marketing professor David Bell kindly recalled the comment, so we had a fun exchange about how I had been living that concept. This transformation from "I" to "we" builds resilience in sales.

Chapter 7

Communication Can Be Complex

"**G**row the love!" was my answer to a question about the purpose of branding in our first-year marketing class. It stuck. "Grow the love" morphed into "J-love" (referring to Section J) and became a common spoken quote and even a slogan for our t-shirts. Twenty years later, I still sign the section update emails "grow the love!" Communication can be clear, simple, direct, and concise. Other times, as kids are fabulous at highlighting, communication can be confusing. My son once asked, "Mom, why do we call them **cow**-boys, when they ride *horses*?" I find that communication (intended as well as unintended) is actually quite complex.

Would you choose to see Katharine Graham or Tony Robbins? Would you choose Jeff Bezos or Allan Gilmour? Dozens of excellent student-run clubs at the Harvard Business School do a phenomenal job of bringing in guest speakers to connect with the students. Tony Robbins leaves standing room only. Yet I chose to hear media icon and women's executive pioneer Katharine Graham share her story at that same moment. When she died two years later, I knew I had made the correct decision for me. In 2017, when Steven Spielberg released the major motion picture *The Post* about Katharine Graham's life, I found it especially enjoyable because I had had the privilege of speaking with her directly.

Similarly, I wanted to hear Ford Motor Company CFO Allan Gilmour talk about his career with the company that shaped my childhood. I also wanted to grasp his perspective about being an openly gay senior executive. So, I took a pass on attending the Jeff Bezos presentation that evening. The year prior, I had been lucky enough to host Jeff Bezos in a small group discussion. There he shared stories of the intimate beginnings of Amazon. I remember him explaining that the name was selected simply because it started with an "A" and needed to be top on the internet search engines Yahoo, Lycos, and AltaVista (Google was not even considered as it was just coming on the scene in 1998). Bezos also described instructing employees to order a certain book at the same time to show demand through the system. I find it helpful to remember that even the megacorporations had humble beginnings.

As a student and club organizer, I was initially frustrated that the killer talks all seemed to take place at the exact same moment. I scheduled an appointment with the administrative room coordinator to file my complaint. What she taught me turned out to be by far the most valuable lesson I learned my entire two years in business school and perhaps one of the most important lessons of my life. I went in with a well-structured argument for why we should be able to schedule Jeff Bezos at 5:00 p.m. and Allan Gillmour at 6:30, for example.

That way, if students wanted to, they could attend both events. Her reply denying my request was not about managing crowds or the size of the available auditoriums.

Matter-of-factly, she stated with confidence, "You are Harvard Business School students. You will always have great options and many demands on your time. Now is as good a time as any to learn that you cannot be in two places at once. We intentionally schedule concurrent sessions so that you can exercise the critical skill of how to best spend your time."

Ouch. Sometimes the best medicine comes as a shot in the arm. That message that day surely did. What she was teaching through the decision to schedule two people at once was more powerful than anything she could have ever said. The purpose of this chapter is not just about being clear with our words—although that is important, and I have some funnies to share in that department. My first goal with this chapter is to invite you to consider your complete communication and its context. I hope you will ask yourself if you are indeed communicating what you intend.

For example, I know dozens of friends who tell their newly licensed teenagers to not text while driving. However, those same parents have been carpooling those same kids around for years, often with a phone in hand and often texting while driving. Texting and driving terrifies me personally, so I decided early I would not be "telling" my kids to refrain from texting while driving. Rather, I would show them. Additionally, I would put them to work learning the habit. There were two parts to the lesson. One is the ability to put down the phone. The other is to have a passenger handle any phone matters.

My middle schooler and all his friends know my car is a no-phone zone. If they want a ride, they have to put down the phone and chat with me. This is not a rule that I even have to share anymore. I love watching either my son or, more often, his main carpool buddy explain to whomever the new rider is "no phone in Ms. Bea's car." These ten or fifteen minutes are the best insights to what they are learning at school, who is likely to make the basketball team, and the like. Most importantly, it is a subtle but powerful reminder that people and relationships matter, and devices can wait.

Secondly, as a sole provider and caregiver, I do have plenty of emails, texts, and voicemails that often require urgent attention. On longer drives, my children learned it was their job to manage my phone while I managed the road. They navigate the map, read and reply to emails, manage payments, answer texts, and so on. This communicates both that my work schedule, not their social calendar, is the priority as well as that the driver should not get distracted by their phone. At one point, I had a business partner who used foul language. So the side benefit of my "traveling administrative assistant technique" was her cleaning up her act when I revealed it was a fourteen-year-old listening to the voicemails.

The worst parenting I have ever witnessed was done by yours truly. We spent an eight-hour day out on a boat with friends. My twelve-year-old came along, thinking it would be a three- or four-hour event. By the end, he was not only tired, but sunburned, hungry, dehydrated, bored, and frustrated. Throughout the day, I had put him in many confusing situations. First, one adult was encouraging him to rest in the shade and relax with a game on his phone, which was the limited option available. Minutes later, another adult scolded him for being on his phone when we were surrounded by the great outdoors (but that he had embraced for six hours). Secondly, several nineteen-year-olds were in the group, and they were freely drinking plenty of alcohol, even though the legal drinking age was twenty-one.

"Why am I not permitted to use my phone for an age-appropriate game, when they are permitted to do illegal activities?" was one of the thoughts scrambling in my son's mind. Good question. I wish the parenting mistakes had ended there. Unfortunately, I was present when the drinking expanded beyond the confines of a private boat to a public restaurant, requiring a fake ID.

What did happen is that the twelve-year-old eventually blew his cool, started acting out, and even was screaming. I met his behavior with a ten-point discipline plan that included an immediate removal from the scene, restrictions from friends and devices in the following weeks, gratitude exercises, and more. Yet, it took me months to do the most important parenting step, which was to apologize. I was terribly wrong to be complicit in such rampant destructive behavior and to be neglectful of his physical state after such a long day. In one situation, I was accidentally communicating exactly the opposite value of what he and I had spoken about for years prior and since.

What are you saying to your colleagues, children, and spouse? Is it what you intend?

Timing matters too. My first boss in an office setting illustrated this perfectly. Michael was particularly good at caring about everyone on the team individually and personally. One day he was coming by my desk informing me, "Hey, I am running into a meeting and need you to answer this prospect's question for me...." As he did, he saw that I was exasperated, as my computer system had crashed and I was under pressure with a major proposal. I was just about to call him in for help. When he saw the situation, he immediately reorganized his priorities, delayed his meeting, assigned someone else to answer the prospect need, and gave his full attention to helping me solve the bigger hitch with my crashed system.

Had he kept his course, he would not have been "wrong." Yet, he would have subtly communicated to me that me and my issues were not that important to him. Instead, he did the opposite. He showed me he valued my time and wanted me to always be able to perform at peak levels. He demonstrated that his role was to ensure I had what was needed to succeed. Since then, I have always remembered that when a senior leader shows subordinates that their time is valuable, then they will want to spend it wisely too. They will be much less likely to waste it in water cooler talk, surfing the internet, and the like.

Good timing is not luck or random. It can be a productively trained habit. Simply commit to greeting your spouse, child, and colleagues with a smile and positive words. Good to do so on departing as well. Me saying "Have a great day!" or "I love you!" are what I want remembered. There is always time in between to address the misspelled word, failed test, or light someone forgot to turn off. Perhaps I might worry that I'll forget an important correction and have to blurt it out immediately, "You forgot to post the image on Instagram when you did it on Facebook," before I say, "Good morning, great to see you!" The unintended message is that one post on Instagram is more important than the employee himself. Ugh!

Clarity does matter and can't be taken for granted. Context can help. My British colleague constantly reminds me of the importance of culture and language differences. Yesterday, she waited in a "queue" to buy a sandwich and later said she searched the "rubbish bin" for a discarded document. By themselves, those terms might be perplexing since I wait in "lines" and take out the "trash." However, in context, her vocabulary made sense.

Context can communicate a relevant message even when the words are dead wrong. My friend Dianne taught me this when she hit me over the head with a brick...figuratively. I didn't often get to see Dianne as she was more of a mommy mentor, living life at a different stage than me. So, when I get the pleasure of rare one-on-one time with her, I treasure it. On this particular day, I was riding a ferry with no kids in tow (a rarity for sure), so we were enjoying a quiet conversation when my phone rang. I saw that it was my mom, and I knew she was about to take a flight, so I interrupted my chat with Dianne, stood on the back of the ferry boat where phone usage was permitted, and answered. My mom restated flight details and plans she had just told me two hours earlier. Basically, it was a content-free exchange. Returning to Dianne, I was annoyed that our time had escaped us. When I shared with her my disappointment, Dianne considered the context and said, "You are so lucky. She wasn't calling you to tell you some facts. She was calling to say that yours was the last voice she wanted to hear before the plane took off."

How we speak matters. How we listen matters more.

Professionally, I learned this as well. My favorite bit of feedback came after a talk I gave on personal branding. The most important message in building authority is that the "riches are in the niches." I often teach that you cannot be all things to all people, so in order to become the recognized expert in a field, make sure the field is very small. Once that is done, it is surprisingly easy to replicate and expand. For example, don't attempt to be the best college counselor in America. Rather, get known as the go-to person for Raleigh, North Carolina, high school athletes seeking an Ivy League education.

Don't attempt to career coach senior-level executives. Rather, become the go-to person for women in their forties seeking to make strides in financial services. So when I received feedback from this talk, "the riches are in the niches" was the most common bit of advice that people appreciated. I have a dozen thank-you notes from people who narrowed their scope as a result and were immediately seeing an improvement with their personal brand.

The best (and funniest) note came from someone who thanked me for my advice that the "riches are in the ditches!" What? This is not only something I never said, it is not even something I would have ever thought. He went on to explain that he appreciated my encouragement to treat every prospect with respect, that we never know from where the next gold mine comes. Now, this was relatable and was a theme throughout my entire talk. So, even though he heard the words incorrectly—some of the actual message was spot on.

I've experienced language difficulties on numerous occasions, so I learned to listen twice when something sounds amiss. Several years ago, our family shared accommodations with British friends on a Disney vacation. My daughter's fifth birthday was that week, so she brought her full Cinderella gown and was planning to wear it to her "Birthday Ball" at the castle. We arrived at our shared villa after a long day of sightseeing and saw our friend's son in the swimming pool. He called out to my daughter, "Hey, your costume is in the toilet!" My daughter and I were aghast as to why someone would put her Cinderella gown in the commode. My blood was boiling. Quickly, I stomped inside to check on the situation. It was only after seeing the gown safely hanging in the closet that I realized our English friend was simply letting us know my daughter's swimsuit (costume) was in the bathroom (toilet).

In his mind, he was offering an invitation, more like, "Come on in, the water is fine." We erupted in laughter when we realized the misunderstanding.

In my work supporting entrepreneurs, we also had to cross cultural boundaries. Seed investors in idea-stage startups are often corporate businesspeople, doctors, or lawyers. Connecting these sorts of successful individuals with entrepreneurs is essential in nurturing a startup community. Helping them get comfortable with the language of startups was an important first step to getting them involved as advisors and investors. Phrases such as minimal viable product, risk capital, private placement memorandum, accredited investor, crowdfunding, and so on may sound foreign to most of us. However, spotting true talent behind a good idea or a hardworking founder is like recognizing a smile—everyone can do it.

The tongue is powerful. It is worth noting that what is said is out there and can't get back inside. A Jewish parable about a gossipmonger and a feather pillow illustrates this point well. The talebearer regrets hurting the reputation of a neighboring businessman by profusely spreading stories, so he attempts to apologize to the town rabbi and the businessman. He is surprised when the rabbi requests that he bring a feather pillow and a knife to the meeting. The rabbi begins the meeting by asking the gossip to slash the pillow with the knife and watch all the feathers fill the air. Then he explains that, like the stories, once the feathers are out, they cannot all be collected back in order to make the pillow like new.

The intense power of the tongue fuels the reality that many of my classmates are remembered by only one or two comments throughout their two years. "It's Hooters in the sky" is one I remember during a class discussion about the business strategy of hiring only attractive flight attendants at Singapore Airlines.

"Grow the love" is the comment that marked me personally. It was made about the importance of branding, and coincidentally, the comment branded me for life. It fits. Love is what I do best. What comments come out of your mouth? Are you aware that those comments are branding you?

My boss Michael provided a great example for me, and in school I got lucky with the comment that "stuck." However, at home I often make mistakes in this department. My son will empty the full dishwasher and before saying "thank you," I comment, "The spatula belongs in this drawer, not that one." Or my daughter will rake piles of leaves and before saying "great job!" I will comment on the correct level to fill the bag. Perfect is indeed the enemy of the good. Way more important than being clear, contextually correct, and complete is language that is complementary. It says, "I care."

Chapter 8

They May Not Remember What You Said, But They'll Never Forget That You Listened

"You came here years ago with a story to tell, you left as world-class listeners," exclaimed one of my professors at our fifteen-year class reunion. He was correct. The case method classroom is a science lab for listening. All aspects of teaching, including the architecture, class rhythm, and grading practices, are impeccably designed around this goal.

The world-class listening skills we learned in the classroom, which I am about to describe to you in detail, are the most important tool of my parenting. That matters because I am a wonderful parent. I must be. Someone recently told me I am. Let's think about it. The word *wonder-ful* means full of wonder. I wonder if my kids have done their homework. I wonder if they are going to eat dinner. I wonder if they will come home on time. I wonder if they will be respectful. Yep, I am a *wonderful* parent.

At my school, even the physical structure of the classroom is designed to provide each student with an excellent listening experience. The almost-semi-circle has tiered seating. Each student has a name card in front of his or her desk which can be read from the front or the back because the architecture of the room is such that everyone is visible. We sat in the same seats every day, only switching once to a newly assigned seat halfway through the year. There are no computer screens for students to hide behind, and there is plenty of room for notes, printed case studies, and such to be laid out at your fingertips for quick reference.

The case method is the cornerstone to the design. Each case is examined for ninety minutes via group discussion of eighty people. Although eighty people sounds like too many to have a meaningful discussion, it wasn't. As I mentioned in the introduction, we were all organized in sections, and thus for the entire first year had all of our classes with the same people, so we knew each other well. This, combined with stellar professor facilitation, made the discussions lively and meaningful.

A side note about the physical structure of the room: we affectionately refer to the top row as the "sky deck," which is knowledge I shared once with my children. So, at a reunion, when my children were invited to study a case and then participate with other children of alumni in a case discussion, my daughter snagged her spot in the sky deck. Therefore, she can say, "I was in the top of my class at Harvard."

The rhythm of the class also builds attentiveness. Each class begins with a "cold call" to one student who is then required to open the day's dialogue with a ten- to fifteen-minute summary of the case. Throughout the class, the professor speaks less than twenty minutes in total, often in thirty-second bits, as a way of prodding students to dig deeper or moving the conversation around the room. Knowing the names, backgrounds, skill sets, and so on of the eighty students present, the professor finds ways to pull relevant and accurate information out of each student. Twenty years later, I am still impacted from watching professors in action after they had clearly read through each of our files. As a result, I now thoroughly research LinkedIn profiles, company websites, and social media prior to every phone call and meeting I have.

Finally, even the grading methodology is structured for excellence in mindfulness. Class participation is the cornerstone of every grade, roughly 40 percent of the final grade. So, silence is not an option...but talking too much isn't an option either. All my student life I was familiar with class participation grades and learned quickly to speak early and often. However, that system did not work at HBS. Here, class participation is more about *listening* than talking. Every comment must carefully build upon what has already been said and needs to logically support or disprove previous comments. Thus, the students are alert for insights, forming questions and looking for opportunities to jump in with relevant contributions.

Whereas "filler" one-liners were shining stars in the "more is better" class participation programs found in high school and even college roundtables, the same sort of "filler" comments in business school were seen as distractions, obvious lame attempts for participation points, and thus counted as deductions in grading. Since you do not know when you will be called, it is imperative that each of the eighty classmates is always prepared for an unsolicited call.

Additionally, we would go on the "offensive" with meaningful comments. We would likely have our hand up five or six times for each one time we were called on to share a comment. Daily, I came to class with a handful of carefully researched and well-thought-through observations from the case. I raised my hand at appropriate times for more than an hour, eager to make a valuable contribution. Yet, very often, by the time I was called upon, the conversation had moved in a direction where my statement would have then been ill-timed or unwelcome. In those moments, active intentional consciousness with quick decision-making skills was honed with a general conclusion that I should reign back my intended monologue and go for a quick word of support and encouragement for the most recent comment. Sometimes less is more. If you are raising a teenager, you know what I mean.

Two bits of encouragement for becoming an effective listener are to listen better and listen longer.

A sweet example of listening better comes from Beaver Cleaver. Do you remember the 1950s family TV show, *Leave It to Beaver*? No, of course you don't (but YouTube can give the context).

The young son Beaver is sitting at the kitchen table with a pen and paper. He looks up for a moment to ask, "Hey mom, what's sex?"

Mother June Cleaver gets very fidgety and a little nervous and starts walking around the kitchen, saying things in a hesitant voice, "Well, you know, Beav, your father and I really love each other, and your father and I are very dedicated to each other. And you know...," she starts talking about the blessings of marriage, and as she speaks, she is squirming. Finally, she says, "Why do you ask?"

Beaver answers simply, "Because I'm filling out this form, and it says sex: *M* or *F*?"

I often make that mistake. I jump in to answer when I'm not even understanding what the question is. It is human nature. Robert, my middle child, who didn't speak a word until he was two, illustrated this for me. Until he was nearly three years old, he was totally bald, had huge brown eyes, and looked like he was always pondering something. He had this little crinkle on his forehead, so throughout his babyhood, we often laughed and asked, "What do you suppose he is thinking?" It was the cutest thing you could imagine.

I would say to him, "Oh, Robert, you are adorable!"

At that point, his vocabulary was obviously limited, so whenever he heard the syllable "a" it was not as part of a larger word but as a modifier to a noun, as in "a desk" or "a lamp." Thus, in response, he would angrily scrunch his brow and snap, "I am not a table!" (Pronounced "TAY-ble.")

There he was, getting mad when I'm giving him a compliment because he is not actually hearing what I'm saying.

At age two, Robert illustrated the importance of listening well. He offered some of the best office and marriage advice I know. A professor, at the fifteen-year reunion, wanted to impart the same wisdom. Repeatedly during the reunion weekend, the instruction was: *be approachable, break down barriers to communication, don't get stuck in the ivory tower.* He assumed in the fifteen years since graduation, the returning alumni may have achieved enough success to gain responsibility, staff, and stature, but they were in the dangerous position of not being told honest feedback. The underlying message was that to get to the next level, honest feedback is required. The higher you rise, the more important and more difficult listening becomes. The major distinction here is not that we only have to listen when someone is trying to speak. We need to be inviting and even innovative about ways to solicit input.

Listening is so critical to success that the skills for doing so need to be honed constantly. The culture of an organization, family, and classroom succeed when effective concentration skills are nurtured. The more you hear feedback, particularly constructive criticism, about your failures, the more you will succeed. Truly, the only way to be smart in your career is to consistently be the "dumbest" person in the room. In my own dynamic environment, interacting with brilliant entrepreneurs who reside on the cutting edge of technology and innovation, I rest in the comfort that I must be learning, as I frequently feel like the dumbest person in the room. At work, the distinction is subtle. At home, especially regarding technology use, the distinction of "dumbest person in the room" is more obvious and sometimes comes with reminders from loving teens.

Listening to Learn and Learning to Listen

I used to hear, *It is not what you know, but who you know.* Today, I believe success is driven not by who you know or what you know but how fast you can learn. A friend of mine is deciding to re-enter her career after an eight-year hiatus. She is concerned drastic changes in the fast-paced startup-technology world will prohibit her ability to restart.

She is right, and she is wrong.

She is right, catching up with all of the changes in processes and technology *could be* difficult. She is wrong, though.

It is not necessary to make up for *all* the years. Tools, trends, and networks relevant today are indeed different, but they actually change every few months. So, at any given time she would only be a few months behind, and to some degree, everyone else is "behind" also.

"Keeping up" should not be my friend's goal. Learning what is relevant today and where trends are going should be her focus. The issue is not what you don't know but how fast you can learn. Since this friend is one of the best listeners I know, I am confident she will learn quicker and better than almost anybody. She already enjoys success in her new career.

Listening Longer

Listening longer is also important, and it is especially critical for sales and negotiating. Regina was by far our best salesperson. At one point, she outperformed all the other four salespeople put together. So I started to tag along on her sales calls and see her magic for myself. She was beautiful and charming, and she did know the product. Yet there was something more. Regina had this ability to just stop and wait. A prospect would ask her something like, "How much does that cost?"

She would wait to answer. She might breathe deep. She would smile. It would get uncomfortable. A few seconds would pass. It felt awkward.

The prospect would jump in with "because I am paying your competitor five thousand," or "my budget is four thousand." They couldn't bear the silence.

Many people, including sales expert and author Brian Tracy, have written about the power of the pause, a planned pause, or awkward silence. People don't like long waits. Regina's ability to wait longer than the other person meant that they would give her information like budgets, decision-making processes, competition, and the likelihood of buying.

Later that year, at the Christmas party, I was talking with Regina's husband, who was, of course, thrilled because she had had a great year. I said, "Harold, Regina is phenomenal!" I went on to explain what I learned about how she waits so well and is incredible with the awkward silence.

Harold explained with a smile, "You know, maybe she didn't *learn* that skill. She actually once fell off a horse and suffered a concussion. So, maybe she just takes her time soaking in conversations, waits as she digests information, and then collects her thoughts." Isn't it interesting when a "disability" becomes an asset? Regardless of the validity of Harold's theory, now Regina is a very wealthy woman who has enjoyed a thirty-year super successful sales career.

There are some tricks and tips for listening longer. First, I time myself to know the length of my natural comfort with a pause. Then I work to increase it. As I sit in a sales or negotiation situation, I actually count in my head. One, two, three, four, I hope they will say the next thing.

Secondly, I envision a round clock during every meeting with a prospect. I keep a tab in my head, making sure that they speak more than I do. I have found the sweet spot is to aim for 60 percent of the time that the prospect is speaking. It's really easy to get them to speak 30 percent of the time and unnecessarily awkward to get them to speak 85–90 percent. If I can strategically allow them to speak 60 percent of the time, I know I am going to close the deal. I am going to hear what they need, what is important to *them*, what it is going to take to close them on the sale. The best way to achieve this is to ditch any list of features and benefits. No one wants a regurgitated list. It is much more effective to wait until the prospect

1 HOUR
ONE ON ONE MEETING

■ TIME I AM TALKING

☐ TIME THE OTHER PERSON IS TALKING (PROSPECT, NEGOTIATION PARTNER, CHILD OR EMPLOYEE)

▨ 3-5 MINUTES WHERE GAME-CHANGER INFORMATION IS SHARED. ALLOWS US TO MOVE TO GREAT THINGS. COMES AFTER TRUST AND CONNECTION!

has expressed a specific frustration or pain. Only after listening carefully and demonstrating true concern, can you then offer the feature or benefit that will solve their issue. The rest of the list is largely irrelevant. Interestingly, if I have a one-hour meeting, and thus the prospect is talking for thirty-five to forty minutes of that time, only about three to five minutes of what they say is important to making the sale. My job is to listen carefully and wait patiently for those three minutes. This skill was Regina's superpower.

Part 3

Practical Business Success Skills

NEGOTIATION —>
GOAT
NATION
TAINTING
NEGATION
TINTING
NETTING
GOTTEN
TANGENT

Chapter 9

Taking the Ego Out of Negotiation

"**I** am the reason for your success," I announced to my friend and section mate more than ten years after graduation. This was quite a proclamation given his incredible achievements. He had been the chief financial officer for several top tech companies. My classmate's curiosity was piqued by my comment, but he is such a humble, kind guy his first reaction was "thank you!" I went on to explain that I was referring to finance class roughly a decade earlier. Our finance professor came from the business school INSEAD in Paris and had a very heavy accent. He not only recognized that I was the least capable finance student, he also didn't like my name. He would wave his hand and complain, "Bea! Bea is not a name. Bee is a pest...*buzzz*," and with more hand motions he would give another *"buzz,"* eventually concluding, "It must be Bay-A. Bay-A is a name." So there I sat, struggling with the financial concepts, and to some degree, also with my own identity.

Brilliant classmates would articulate why the case protagonist should or should not buy the company in question, or to what degree the corporation valuation was reasonably calculated, or whether the loan, leveraged buyout, sale, or divestiture was a wise decision. Our professor would interrupt their sophisticated arguments to ask, "But can Bay-A understand that? Speak to the class in a way that Bay-A can understand."

I explained to my pal that as a CFO handling countless acquisitions, his financial acumen, spreadsheet proficiency, and market valuation wisdom were only part of the skills needed. What really mattered was the ability to make the founder comfortable when selling his or her company. Founders literally see and refer to their startups as their "babies." After all, they have dedicated their lives to create a viable company in a competitive high-paced market. How else would they be far enough in the process to even speak to tech giants about acquisition. Even though acquisition is the endgame for the founder, letting go of the "baby" is never easy.

Speaking in high-falutin' vocabulary about fancy spreadsheets would intimidate the seller, sour the relationship, and thus squander the deal. However, talking through terms and conditions in everyday language is the key to a successful negotiation. Together we laughed remembering, ...*but would Bay-A understand*? I claimed that my weakness was the reason for his success.

I took a negotiation course, which focused on three major skills needed to build strong relationships. The first part of building relationships, as the previous story illustrates, is relatability. Another important aspect is to seek a win-win result. In order to do so, we must relinquish our tendency to approach a negotiation with a zero-sum proposition. The first step is to approach the other party with a vision of what success looks like for them instead of what I want to get out of the deal. Converging in agreement must create something greater than the sum of its parts. Visually, the common image of tug of war with a compromise in the middle must be rejected. A more productive visual is a medium pizza cut in half. Rather than aiming to get one more slice from my partner's side, I think about ways that connecting allows us to grow our medium pizza into a large.

Creating a win-win versus zero-sum mentality is also a daily practice when raising children. I enjoy having William fold the clothes for the whole family. He likes extending his TV privileges. Often, one more basket of clothes means watching a whole additional episode of *The Office*.

BATNA still is my favorite lesson from that class. BATNA means Best Alternative To Negotiated Agreement, which is basically a fancy way of saying, *always be willing to walk away*. For example, if you are seeking a new career or job opportunity, never bother to have just one option. There is no reason to do the work just to create a linear path which ends up leaving you vulnerable and at the mercy of whomever is potentially making you an offer. Rather, always work two or more options in parallel. This is necessary not just for negotiating *in* the deal but is the only way to know you are on the right path, being reasonable. And it will help your conversation and keep you confident.

I travelled with my children for three months in Australia. Admittedly, I overspent on our travel excursions, so I needed work as soon as we returned. I knew that pursuing one lead would not do the trick. I worked multiple leads and scheduled Skype interviews often at 2:00 a.m. Australia time. Our flight landed in Savannah, Georgia, at 11:00 p.m. on December 12th. The next morning, I reported two hours up the road in Charleston for six hours' worth of final third-round interviews. By the 15th, I was in Atlanta for similar all-day interviews with a selection committee. By Christmas I had two job offers in hand and started work on January 2nd in Charleston. I am convinced I would not have secured either position unless I had been working on both...securing my BATNA.

Even before I was taught the phrase BATNA during my MBA, HBS served for all intents and purposes *as* my BATNA. In chapter 1, I explained how I applied and was accepted one year earlier than anticipated. "Congratulations! You are part of a very exclusive club, those who have been accepted to Harvard Business School!" The chairman of the board offered his praise. He continued, "How would you like to be a part of an even more exclusive club?"

I couldn't imagine what he meant.

"Those who turn down Harvard Business School."

At that time, I was the west coast sales manager, and I was responsible for the majority of the company's annual $5 million revenue. The three owners were positioning the company for acquisition and thus searching for a new CEO. The current CEO was the founder and a major shareholder. He sought to depart upon acquisition. We needed to demonstrate the company could still thrive without his leadership in order to secure the highest valuation for the company.

Up until that moment, the owners had not considered promoting a twenty-seven-year-old sales manager to leapfrog over four senior executives to become CEO. However, now that my acceptance letter served as a prime BATNA in hand, they couldn't afford to lose me (and my sales). After two weeks of deliberating and meeting with all three owners, I indeed turned down my admission to HBS and accepted the role as one of Silicon Valley's youngest female CEOs. (Two years later, after we were acquired by a public company, I chose to reapply...this time, the GMAT *was* required.)

In summary, I was taught that to win *in* a negotiation you have to look outside the negotiation to build the relationship, grow the potential for both sides, and build an alternative. These rules apply when raising children.

Naturally, nurturing the relationship and building trust is paramount. My son struggled with his behavior, particularly respecting adults. He muttered things under his breath around teachers and coaches. Worse, sometimes he talked back to them with inappropriate language and tone.

I established rules against bad behavior and rewards for good behavior. That made no impact on solving the problem. To the contrary, his conduct became more exaggerated and he became exasperated with me.

Finally, I took time to really learn how he felt and understand what was going on inside. We made some progress. In almost every case, William was correctly expressing a valid concern. A teacher may have misjudged a situation having come into the room late and missing most of the troubling scene; a coach gave too little playing time to a deserving teammate, or a referee made many bad calls. I began to recognize that on a scale of one to ten, the *infraction* William observed was about a two or three. However, his *reaction* was about a six or seven. I started to describe to him how his overreaction to the situation brought attention to him and not the situation. This resulted in William having the opposite impact of what he hoped. I pointed out, "You are smart, capable, and articulate. The world needs you to have a voice. When you behave like that, you in reality mute yourself and invalidate the very problem you seek to remedy." By digging deeper and validating his feelings and needs, I negotiated for a much-improved demeanor.

With my children, I keep the principle but edit some of the rules when it comes to BATNA. I basically play hardball and bring to life the WATNA (worst alternative to negotiated agreement) in order to get the outcome I desire. "You can either get along with the basketball coach or you can switch to playing clarinet." "In the car, we can have meaningful conversation with no cell phone usage, or you will get stuck on the long school bus ride." My personal favorite is clarifying with my teenagers that they can kiss me and hug me in the privacy of our home. If not, when I am at school in front of all their classmates and teammates, I will call out, "I love you, sweetie pie...hope that cute blonde you like talks to you today!" They know I would do it, and thus they never leave without me getting the affection I desire.

So, for the most part, the principles business school teaches around negotiation work well with children. Additionally, as a parent, I learned that winning *in* the negotiation is dependent upon setting the stage outside of the negotiation. I learned to establish myself as the boss, to create an acceptable negotiation field, and to create two options I love.

The first, establishing the parent as the boss, seems obvious. However, in today's culture, the opposite is true. I will say more about this in chapter 16: Write Your Ticket. So, for now, I will only address the language around establishing the parent as the boss, which has changed drastically in America through the generations. My parents were raised when children were to be seen and not heard. They were well dressed with starched collars. They waited until they were addressed to speak, and even then, it was quite limited and likely only a word of obedience. This was ideal for the industrial time period and a manufacturing economy where union workers perform specific, often repetitive, duties as required.

By the late sixties, I was raised to have minimal input. My parents informed me how my day would be spent, what we would eat for dinner, and they set expectations regarding homework and chores. I did have the chance and was even encouraged to contribute to the dinner conversation, and I could make limited choices. This sort of input worked well to prepare me for a more innovative economy where visionary CEOs set a direction and then encouraged individuals to contribute creatively within their purview.

It is common for today's children, even toddlers, to be bombarded with questions they couldn't possibly answer. We don't tell two-year-olds that they are going to the aquarium today and will be having lunch at Chick-Fil-A. Rather, we ask them all day,

"Do you want to go to the park? The pool? The aquarium?"

"Do you want to have lunch at the chicken or the pizza place?"

"Do you want to eat on the red or blue plate?"

"Do you want to wear shorts?"

We are unintentionally and consistently reinforcing that the two-year-old is the boss. Then we are shocked when they have a temper tantrum or don't listen when we ask something of them. We even have the nerve to refer to them as the "terrible twos." It is no surprise that this sort of narrative pattern has led to many youngsters struggling to conform to the demands of gainful employment.

I spent an afternoon with my then-three-year-old and one of my friends who has not raised children. My friend asked the three-year-old about ten questions, always allowing her to make the decisions about going to the park, swinging, and so on. The eleventh question, "Will you please wash up for dinner?" was sadly met with a tantrum. So, I looked at the pattern and I learned. I decided it was okay to give her her way when she was making a reasonable request like, "May I have some grapes?" Yet, I edited my "yes" answer to also include my own request like, "Let's say the alphabet with each grape we eat. I will begin with the letter A." In doing so, I set a healthy rhythm to our conversation. It is a subtle and consistent reminder that I am the one in charge.

Creating an acceptable field for negotiation is a second practice my children made me learn. Rather than argue with them about touching items in the grocery store, my bestie taught me to set boundaries. We declared they could touch up to twenty items but could only do so with their pinky finger.

Most importantly, my children made me learn to create two options, both of which I loved. They can either fold the clothes or empty the dishwasher before I drive them to basketball. This lesson has been most impactful in my sales career. I never work with a prospect who is considering one solution I am selling. To do so would be to ask the question, "Yes or no?" I prefer to be presenting two potential solutions and thus ask, "Which one is best for you, the monthly or annual contract?"

Chapter 10

Focus Makes You Unique in Today's Scattered World

I hope you are so far loving this book about our Sunday sailing adventures...*just kidding*...checking in to see that you are still focused and paying attention.

In year one, I studied the famous Jack Stack case. The case protagonist, Jack Stack, was a young executive with International Harvester, a huge company on its way to bankruptcy. Stack was sent to the Springfield, Missouri, manufacturing facility basically to shut it down and lay off all the employees because the company was hemorrhaging money. However, when he started working there, Stack fell madly in love with the wonderful team and decided he wanted to save their jobs, as well as his own, of course. He saw that they were doing great work. Stack really paid attention when employees asked him very personal questions like "should I take out a credit card? Have a baby? Obtain a mortgage?" They looked to him as the manager who could see into the black box of the future and know about their financial security.

Unfortunately, for a long time, the books had been revealing that the company was getting deeper into trouble. And the books did not lie. However, the factory employees were not engrossed in the numbers as they had no direct knowledge of the financials and no real access to the reports. Stack changed all that. After knocking on the doors of over fifty banks seeking a $9 million loan, Stack became economically literate. He learned to speak the language of finance, understand the balance sheet, calculate financial ratios, and project when money would be paid back.

The location which had been the International Harvester ReNew Center was spun out to become Springfield ReManufacturing Corporation (now SRC Holdings Corporation). Stack insisted that every employee learn how the business operated and how it made money. He wanted them to review the balance sheet themselves and then decide whether they should have a child, take out a credit card, get a mortgage, and so on.

Changing the center of attention changed the company and the lives of over 119 families. Laser focus on financial reporting secured the financial health of the company.

Stack went on to pioneer the open-book management leadership model and author *The Great Game of Business* and *A Stake in the Outcome*. Stack teaches others how to engage teams in detailed weekly meetings exploring the corporation's financial health through metrics and reporting systems.

Alan Mulally saved Ford Motor Company with a similar style with a focal point on the numbers. His famous business plan review (BPR) meetings were always held on the same day, at the same time, and in the same place with mandatory attendance for Ford's senior executives. Mulally used a color-coded red, yellow, and green system to target which metrics were failing, potentially behind, or on track. I particularly love the color coding because I know that zooming in on the yellow of the tennis ball has saved dozens of matches for me. Similarly, when my son seems intimidated by defenders blocking his shots, directing his attention to the orange of the rim is a helpful nugget.

For several years, I had the pleasure of working for ForbesBooks where the CEO, Adam Witty, was a huge Alan Mulally fan. So naturally, we also had weekly BPRs and spent significant time thinking about the numbers. I am so grateful for that experience and the wisdom I gained in those times. Amazingly, as a ForbesBooks executive, I was invited to speak for a Forbes Small Giants event. There, I had the thrill of meeting Jack Stack's co-author Bo Burlingham. Don't you just love when life comes full circle like that? I know I do!

As a matter of fact, that company afforded me another spectacular full-circle moment. Adam had a way of doing in stride what others might consider unimaginable. One such thing was flying Alan Mulally to Charleston, South Carolina, for a meeting. I personally had no prior knowledge of him coming. So, imagine my surprise (and delight) when the smiling redhead casually walks into my downstairs office to engage in a detailed conversation about my father's thirty-three-year career with Ford Motor Company. It was the single most exciting moment of my professional career. Lucky me!

At home, the Jack Stack and Alan Mulally lessons about measurable targets made an impact as well. I had watched a love of basketball blossom in my son. He played constantly, however there was not a consistent improvement in line with the number of hours he was dedicating to the sport. That is, until he began to focus. Rather than shooting random shots for two hours, we put bright pink masking tape down in one spot in the driveway. Robert would shoot thirty shots just from this spot. At first he would resist, "Mom, this is silly. I won't only shoot from one spot on the court." Or, "How do I know I would get open at this spot." Nevertheless, I told him to make thirty shots or no dinner.

Initially, he had to shoot about fifty in order to make thirty from that spot. By the next week, he would make thirty out of about forty-two. Over the month, Robert would see continued improvement until he was confident in 95 percent success. Once that disciplined concentration was used to hone his shot, he could move to other areas of the court and successfully shoot. His rhythm and form adjusted to the new positions naturally.

More importantly, Robert saw that with intentional time invested, his skill improved. He also learned that he is in control. Improvement is not random. My favorite result of this exercise was a conversation I had with Robert a little while later. I shared that someday he will love a job and profession as much as he loves basketball. "The same way you feel about trying new things, working harder, reading up on stats, et cetera, about basketball, is how you someday will feel about medicine, engineering, computers, or whatever you choose."

What I learned from watching Robert I was able to bring to my career in sales management. The big lesson, believe it or not, wasn't how much he improved from that one spot. The big lesson came from first fixating on that spot and then, once proficiency was achieved (and only *after* proficiency was achieved), moving around the court to practice other shots. There I saw the major improvement in the other locations.

Isolating the shot removed a variable, much like a science experiment aims to do. When Robert was shooting from one marked spot, he would change his momentum, knee bend, arc of the shot, elbow position, and such in order to improve. As those things were perfected, the variable of position could be reintroduced.

As a sales manager, I bring that lesson with me. Whenever someone is starting out in sales, I try to limit the activity to a very narrow scope. We have a scripted cold call, a templated draft email, and a defined field of potential clients. This gives us the opportunity to review and see what is working and what needs to be changed.

Amazingly, while I am writing this chapter on focus, my colleague Kelly has been reaching out to various groups about me being the speaker for luncheons or meetings that they host. Fortunately, Kelly is deliberate in her approach and, like Robert, is pretty much taking "shots" from one spot on the driveway, so to speak. When she was reaching out to business school alumni associations, they tended to want me to come and speak immediately, months before the book would be in hand and with not enough time to make the trip as fruitful as we would like. So Kelly is able to adjust and edit the largely templated email in order to open a conversation about a later date.

On the other hand, Kelly also reached out to Vistage CEO peer groups. The chairs of these organizations tend to plan speakers fifteen months in advance. So Kelly altered her "shot" accordingly. Had Kelly just been randomly connecting with a variety of potential audiences, she would never have been able to learn the patterns of each and meaningfully adjust to serve them better.

My professors also taught focus when they talked about muscle memory. Interestingly, Srikant Datar would use the basketball free throw analogy. He wanted us to know that the term did not apply only to physical tasks. Srikant encouraged us to also exercise muscle memory when it came to our own moral compass which was all about making thoughtful key decisions over and over until "doing what is right" became a habit. Building such moral muscle is training the brain.

Mel Robbins knows all about training the brain. Her book *The 5 Second Rule* sold millions of copies. It is not about the dirt on the floor and the forgiveness you are granted if your child picks up his lollypop after dropping it on the floor and starts eating it.

Rather, Robbins's *5 Second Rule* is based on her personal revival, which all started with the need to change her own habits and retrain her own brain. When she didn't rocket out of bed immediately, she started counting backwards, like NASA does for takeoff. She teaches us to do the same: five... four...three...two...one. Doing so turns off the built-in protective thoughts we have to keep us comfortable, under the covers in bed, pouring that habitual drink, sheltered from change, and so on. We need to first turn off the narrative we play in our heads which binds us to the familiar, so that we can take the actions to get out of bed, make the scary phone call, get dressed for the gym, or kindly confront a loved one.

She is right. For most of us, if we are waiting to feel motivated, it will never happen.

How do we train our brains to work for us and not against us? As I think about her rule more, I realize there are two kinds of people. Those who are seeking that prod to do what they need. And then there are those of us who might be too fast on the gun.

We shoot, then aim. Jump, then wonder about the parachute. We drive, then figure out when we are going.

Which one are you?

At age thirteen, I decided to take up running. Unlike most people Mel Robbins describes, I set my alarm for 6:00 a.m. and, in fact, sprung out of bed. I laced my shoes, popped a Bruce Springsteen, Eagles, and Boston mixtape into my yellow sports Walkman and pushed the "play" button to hear "More than a Feeling." The breeze was flowing, my heart was pumping, I was in my groove. I enjoyed passing the gorgeous homes and trees in our suburban neighborhood as I made a big loop. Cheering myself on at 6:45 in the morning as I passed my friends' houses, I was looking forward to bragging about my accomplishment an hour later when we would all meet up on the school bus. I made the final left towards home, and the adrenaline was really flowing. On the slight downhill slope, my step had an extra pep.

It was garbage day. So throughout my run I had seen that most neighbors had pulled their cans to the street. Yet I hadn't thought much about it. However, as I approached my finish at full speed, I was charged. Midway down the hill in front of me were three cans next to each outer. They looked smallish in the distance.

I thought about Evel Knievel. He could easily soar over them and ten others on his motorcycle. "I can take them!" I thought. Running wasn't good enough. I needed a hurdle. As I got closer, the cans got larger. My brain did not adjust to the reality that I had not leapt over anything in my life and perhaps three lined-up trash cans was not the first logical attempt. I sped up. I got more excited. The trash cans got bigger still!

I went for it—right leg in front, left bent behind. It didn't matter that I didn't clear all three full-sized trash cans with both legs. I don't think I cleared even one with my one leg. Three very loud trash cans and I rolled down the hill. (Remember metal trash cans? Well, they were louder than the plastic version you see today.) Here is a bit of advice for you. If you decide you want to try your hurdling skills by leaping trash cans, consider doing so after the truck has come by and emptied them, not before when they are still full of everything you never want to know...or roll down a hill alongside.

Yes, it is handy that my brain might need less retraining than others need in order to get started. However, if I am not properly directed, I can get myself into trouble. I have to be very careful not to "chase squirrels" as my husband likes to remind me. Speaking of my husband, I am thankful that he answered the preacher's critical question with "I do!" even though I had started my personalized wedding vows with "I promise to never tell you a story in a straight line." My ADD has led to plenty of laughs and even some great adventures. Yet, when it comes to business, it is especially crucial for me to have a cornerstoned plan. Jumping and then wondering about the parachute is not a business strategy.

What about you? Are you centered on the right aspects of your business? Unfortunately, it's very easy to lose direction as an entrepreneur, so we are going to solve that problem together. First, a minute defining it. There is always so much to do. Every task is useful, good, and necessary. Often, every task feels urgent. So we run from one to the next. As a result, we can often feel out of control and be left wondering if all that work had any positive results. What I am talking about here, especially for entrepreneurs, gets disguised as an organization competency problem. So, in chapter 12, we will dive deep into efficiency. However, here what I am exploring is more than a productivity issue. I am talking about the challenge of focus, and you, my friend, are about to receive my favorite visual nugget.

Many entrepreneurs think of their total time as a pie and each of the critical tasks as a slice of the pie. Whether they would articulate it like that or not, you might hear them say, "I spend 30 percent of my time on...." Knowing how we spend our time is, as a matter of fact, a great idea, and the pie visual can be a helpful illustration. However, thinking of it in this manner has its risks. As stress and demands increase, more (and thinner) pie-piece slices are added. Deciding how to allocate our talents, investments, and energy can start to resemble a roulette wheel. We are spinning and wherever the marble lands, that is where we spend our energy.

Have you ever felt like that?

I hope none of us will ever feel that way again, it stinks. My best trick to avoiding the roulette-wheel management style is to draw a new circle. It can be the same size. Same number of hours in the day. Same amount of dollars to invest. This time, don't slice the pie. Rather, put the most essential activity right in the center. Then draw additional concentric circles, one for each activity. Concentrate first on that one thing in the center. When that is right, celebrate the victory! Everything else is secondary. For an entrepreneur, this often means cash flow is at the center. For a parent, it is the child's health and safety.

But, how do you figure out what should be the center? And then, how do you build out from there and actualize it? The first challenge is understanding where you are. The second is determining where you are going. For example, if you are sitting on $2 million of cash and your investors are expecting you to be first to market with a stellar product, research and development might initially be more important than making a sale.

Alternatively, you might be more like one of my recent clients launching a consulting firm. Certainly, someday she envisions a beautiful website, slick marketing, a branding package, and scalable operations systems. However, at the time of launch, she has enough cash for three months' expenses *or* cash to invest long term in the business, not both. Fortunately, she also has two paying clients that are covering the bills. So the cash reserve serves more as a three-month safety net than it does a very limited runway. I love the term "runway" because it is so visual for a business startup. It is the space (usually defined by amount of available cash divided by monthly expenses, or burn rate) that a startup has to take off. Yes, I hope you envision your plane soaring.

Let's think about this client's circles. Her pie chart could be a very busy roulette wheel consisting of prospecting phone calls, networking meetings, content writing for marketing and public relations, serving current clients, company formation documentation, and so on. Should she bounce around like a marble, landing randomly on whichever task is present when the wheel stops? Definitely not. As she draws her activities in concentric circles and decides which tasks get the spotlight, she must not only consider where she is and where she is going as stated above. Additionally, she must ask what activities build momentum and which ones drain her energy? Finally, she should consider how much time each one takes.

Considering emotional energy is relevant, even though it is often ignored. For example, I am personally okay with plodding along steadily and only as needed when it comes to legal contracts. I don't feel the need to have them all in place

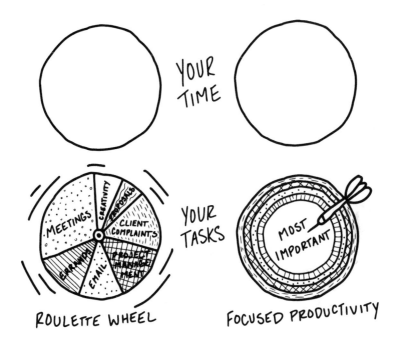

YOUR TIME

YOUR TASKS

ROULETTE WHEEL (MEETINGS, CREATIVITY, PROPOSALS, CLIENT COMPLAINTS, PROJECT MANAGEMENT, EMAIL, BRANDING)

FOCUSED PRODUCTIVITY (MOST IMPORTANT)

ahead of time. Other people would be stressed out about the prospect of someday hiring a contractor or signing on a client without previously working through all the p's and q's of the respective legal jargon. So, when those people establish their concentric circles, they would place a greater priority than I would on having pre-approved legal agreements ready to go.

On the other hand, I know what it is like to slide coins across the gas station countertop hoping to secure enough fuel to make it home. For me, cash is king! So, I will prioritize serving the paying clients so that I can maintain the three-month margin and hedge against something going wrong.

It is important to note that I am not condoning signing bad legal agreements *or* running out of cash. In the illustration above, neither of these things transpire. What I am bringing to the forefront is that energy matters. So knowing yourself and where you are likely to waste time worrying about getting too close to the verge of your personal limits can inform how you effectively spend your resources.

Finally, let's peel this onion back one more layer to investigate how much time tasks genuinely take to complete. This will help us answer questions like, "Do I literally stay in the core until I secure my cash flow (in my example)? Not exactly. Considering the entrepreneur who could consult with two paying clients in order to secure cash flow, we realized that serving these two clients required about twenty-five hours a week of her time. So, my recommendation is certainly to schedule those twenty-five hours as paramount each week. Then I suggest investing the remaining fifteen to twenty hours of work into projects with more long-term impact, whether that be finalizing the website or attending networking events with prospective clients.

Focus doesn't need to mean limiting yourself or your company to only one thing. It can be the tool that illuminates your most high-yielding path.

"Don't you love being pregnant?" An older woman asked me when I was carrying my last child. At first, I thought she might be kidding. I was hot. My back hurt. My two toddlers were relentless about wanting to be picked up. Then she said, "I loved being pregnant. Even if I did nothing else all day, I was producing something." Pregnant women have undeniably clear concentric circles. It is time we give ourselves credit for hitting the bull's-eye just living out those days!

Below are two circles for your convenience. They both represent the same amount of time and the same number of tasks. On the left, please draw pie pieces and label them with your main activities, making the activity that takes up most of your time the largest pie piece. The other pie piece sizes should be proportional to the time you spend on those items. On the right-hand circle, please draw concentric circles, the exact same number of circles as you have pie pieces on the left. Make your most imperative activity your label for the center circle. Each subsequent surrounding concentric circle should be labeled for your other activities, in diminishing order of most meaningful to least vital.

Ready? Don't overthink this, just get started. Five, four, three, two, one. Let's go!

Chapter 11

Collaboration and Delegation
KNOWING WHEN TO TEAM UP AND KNOWING WHEN TO LEAD!

My business school didn't just give lip service to the concept of delegation—it practically forced it on its students. Great institutions don't simply "teach" that delegation is an important aspect of effective leadership. Nor do they instruct students on how to assign work and trust that it will be completed with excellence. Instead, they create situations for students to *experience* delegation.

For example, I was assigned far more work than any one person could possibly handle alone. So, literally everyone forms study groups. They are not assigned officially by the school. It is just a practice done in the culture.

I remember fondly the first few days on campus. Students came up to one another and asked the typical questions:

"What is your name?"

"Where are you from?"

"Do you have a study group yet?"

A what? I thought.

Forming a study group wasn't something I had previously considered. Yet many of my fellow students had had siblings, colleagues, and friends who were alumni. So they knew the inside scoop, so to speak. They explained to me that everyone meets an hour before class over breakfast to discuss the day's cases. At the beginning of the week, the team looks ahead to the course curriculum and assesses the caseload for the week. Together they assign each case to one member of the study group. Everyone will read each case, but one member will really dive deep into the background, analysis of the numbers, research, and so on. That person compiles helpful note sheets for the entire study group.

So, the first week, classmates were busily "recruiting" members as they prepared for the workload soon to come. When I say recruiting, I am not exaggerating. The ideal study group was large enough to distribute the work, but small enough for an intimate conversation, so four or five people. Additionally, it was balanced with different perspectives (such as gender, geography, industry background, or skill set).

One critical question was, "does the group have at least one quant jock?" (Pssst, that means someone excellent at running the numbers.) As luck would have it, my group had a superstar. My roommate could not only crunch dozens of calculations, she always seemed to know which two or three lines from three pages of financial reports were most relevant. Then she would, with a humble smile, say something down to earth like, "See, of course the stock is overpriced because in order to justify the current price, they would need to add a new store a week, which is unlikely." Bam! Immediately, what had been a mysterious black box to me was illuminated. Being able to exchange perspectives and learn intimately from someone else's experience is transformative. Funny, I recently noticed that in her current bio, she says, "I love talking with students about retail apparel research as well as demystifying the analytics behind any comprehensive commentary." Study group relived, I'd say!

My roommate was certainly an ace in the hole when it came to study group participation.

As it happens, the whole group was incredible, and they became some of my dearest friends. Since then, we have shared weddings, funerals, even godchildren.

As for me, I felt more confident with the marketing, personal leadership, or ethics sort of cases. Yet, I crumbled with pressure on the rare occasions that I was trusted with the study group's FRC (financial reporting and control) notes. So much so that each time involved some degree of crying. Apparently, every time I sat at my desk to prepare the financial reporting and control notes and spreadsheets, I cried so hard that even from behind someone could see my shoulders visibly moving up and down. One time when I was surprisingly not doing homework but was laughing at a joke someone had sent by email, I was laughing so hard my shoulders shook. My husband came up the stairs, saw me, and said, "Oh no, not FRC again!"

So study groups were a way of life. They were the first "lesson" in delegating. We learned how to 1) count on other people, 2) establish and articulate the specific responsibilities of each person, and 3) appreciate that we are all much stronger as a team than any one of us could have been as an individual.

But what made that experience "delegation done right"? I believe it is the proactive nature and the great sense of trust. Hundreds of times I have heard company founders, CEOs, and managers say something like, "I am so worn out, I need to delegate!" I have said it myself...and perhaps you have too. They (we) proceed to dump a project onto an unsuspecting (and often ill-prepared employee) until the assignment fails. At which point, the leader inevitably wrongly concludes, "See, I guess I just have to do everything myself."

Thus, the spiral continues where the leader is more worn out, less effective, and unavoidably more desperate. Therefore, the next time he or she repeats, "I am so worn out, I need to delegate" the outcome is even worse.

In these very common situations, the leader is giving delegation about as much thought as "my grocery list is too long for the items to fit in a basket, I think I will get a push cart" as if there is a ready supply of identically capable task-doers lined up to carry the load. There is little to no thought invested in putting that relief system in place.

At home, I constantly delegated tasks to my kids—not because I had the forethought, but because I simply didn't have the bandwidth to handle everything myself. I remember one particular day when I was typing the information to register one of my kids for soccer. I looked across the room and saw the same child playing a video game. Up until that moment, I believed that an adult had to do things like enter data, whereas a child could "learn" from twenty minutes of screen time. A new family rule was born: when you are old enough to register yourself, then—and only then—can you engage in an activity, sport, or what have you.

Forms were the new video game! From that moment on, I've never registered any of my kids for anything! I've never filled out a doctor's form, and I've never filled out paperwork for school. In this age of "affluenza," I found the more I invited my children to do for themselves, two things happened. First, they began appreciating all the little things that I do for them. Second, they practiced their reading and writing while picking up some important data like our address and phone number as well as eventually the list of common questions at a doctor's office.

Mostly, I love that this sort of task delegation for my children reinforced an independent confidence in their own abilities. As they have grown into the teen years, the "leap" to obtaining jobs, researching colleges, and applying for scholarships has been reasonably smooth. I believe that is at least in part because the kinks associated with filling out endless forms have had years to flatten.

This chapter offers two main tenets around delegation. One is building people up. The other is breaking tasks down.

Building others up generally involves a big stretch of that individual's talents and a canvas for personal growth. It is often motivated by a great opportunity. My fifteen-year-old daughter illustrated this principle when I mistakenly informed her that we would spend the majority of our three-month trip to Australia in one small beach town. "No, Mom," she said. "We're not going to stay in one location. If we're going to the other side of the world, we're going to explore." She opened up her screen to display that, unbeknownst to me, she had been compiling a thoughtful list of thirty-two incredible national parks, cliff jumps, waterfalls, and hikes all throughout Australia.

She was determined. So I sat down and shared with her our budget and the login for my Airbnb account. We also set some boundaries around the travel, like that I wouldn't drive more than five hours any one day. Remember, Australia is one big country. Savannah then dedicated the next month to planning each travel and accommodation detail, which included three flights, six thousand miles of driving, and a twenty-five-hour luxury train ride through the Outback. She handled each of the reservations down to the detail of ensuring that free Wi-Fi access was included so we could all keep up with online school and work respectively. Naturally, when we arrived at each of the fourteen accommodations, I was the adult obtaining the key. The owner reached out to shake my hand saying, "Welcome, Savannah, great to meet you!" I was unsure whether I should be embarrassed or proud when I corrected them, introducing Savannah as the fifteen-year-old standing by my side.

Side Note:

Let's take a break from delegation for a moment for me to provide some context, please. A three-month trip to Australia sounds pretty extravagant, and I don't want you to get the wrong idea. We are not wealthy...remember the $700,000 of personal debt...sole provider and caretaker of three kids...we are blessed, more fortunate than most, but not wealthy. So how and why did we go to Australia? Good question. I had recently left a very demanding and structured job due to risky conflicts of interest and an even more risky and increasingly more intolerable long commute. With a little bit of freedom and flexibility, I invested in a luxury magazine and worked remotely with my team ten states away. I had a few months to give it a try before I would have to secure another "real job."

Simultaneously, the lease on our rental home was coming due, so I spoke to the agent about renewing and I had a few questions. He was rude, disrespectful, and utterly uninterested in my concerns. My thought, "How much money does he not want?" Up until that moment, it had never dawned on me to not provide a constant home for my family. Whereas I regularly "deprive" my children of the latest fashions and expensive excursions, food and shelter were non-negotiables that I have been fortunate enough to provide. Yet his demeanor enlightened me. It was just enough of a trigger to move my mind out of the proverbial box of thinking, "we live in this house, we love the neighborhood, I must renew the lease."

I asked myself again, "How much money does he not want?" Then and there I started to calculate not the monthly rent, but I contemplated three months' worth of rent. At that time, I was really not doing it for myself and where I might go, I was thinking it would take him three months to find another long-term tenant (I was right, by the way). Anyway, I tallied three months' rent and added on "savings" of no TV cable and no electricity. Eventually, I saw that if we moved out of our home for four months and put items in storage, a significant sum in excess of $12,000 would not be spent.

The question, "How much money does he not want?" morphed into, "What could I do with $12,000?" It was about to be winter in the US, so my mind began to wander. Turns out Australia offers an eighty-nine-day tourist visa with almost no hassle, online school was readily available and a free option for each of my children, and plane tickets for all of us totally flexible with dates (and two being covered by frequent flyer miles) were less than $4,000. We literally moved out of our home for four months visiting friends and family prior to the trip and enjoying the Christmas holidays two weeks after the trip. We had to go without the fixed cost of a home long enough to be able to amortize the travel costs.

A trip of a lifetime was born! It is not true that I took my family to Australia. Rather, they took me. They are the ones that largely had to purge our consumerism excess to Goodwill, pack up the house, and move boxes into storage. I am forever grateful to that grumpy man who taught me to question that which at first glance seems unquestionable.

Back to Delegation:

Breaking tasks down can sometimes need to be more granular than initially anticipated. It must always be defined by the task or project doer and not by the leader. In other words, as leaders and delegators, we have to meet people where they are. My son's required completion of a cursive writing workbook the summer prior to third grade exemplified my need to meet him where he was and then to grow from there.

To me, cursive was easy. It was fast. So as the summer was winding down, each afternoon I asked Robert to go to his room and do some of his cursive workbook. It never dawned on me to give him detailed instructions about tracing the letters or how far along he should get each day. Every day he dutifully sat at his desk while I prepared dinner, cleaned up the toddler from the beach, and so on. This went on for weeks. So, imagine my shock when I finally did look at the workbook only to find that it was *empty*.

Robert hadn't in truth been disobedient. He was frozen. For weeks he looked at his workbook and each day tensed up at the thought of having to complete the whole thing. So, I asked him to work only on one page. We discussed ignoring the rest of the book. I assured him that completing one page was a great accomplishment. Yet, one page was still too much. Eventually, I encouraged him to attempt only one line.

He only relaxed when I established that completing just the letter *a* was, in fact, a success.

To this day, even when I am working on complex long-term projects involving dozens of people, this experience helps me. We will be reviewing multifaceted Gantt project management charts. At each task, I am thinking (and even hearing in my head) "just trace the *a*, just trace the *a*" as I contemplate whether or not each task is appropriately delegated and communicated to ensure successful completion. As I break down tasks for team members, I am grateful my son taught me to meet people where they are.

Obtaining referrals for any business is a great illustration of how powerful it can be to break tasks down. When you ask friends, family, and adoring clients to refer business to you, how much success do you have? If you are like most, even with contacts who are willing and supportive, it is only about two or three people out of a hundred that will actually make an introduction. I don't love those odds. Breaking down the tasks is the key environment for getting great referrals.

The first step in breaking it down is to give people something to say or even forward. I encourage clients to have a standard short informative email. It should include something like, "Thanks for caring to introduce me to people I can help...we typically serve _____ organizations. We can help by offering _____." The email should not be overwhelming with attachments or data, but a link to a website can be helpful. Doing this simple step, I saw referral numbers go from about 3 percent to 35 percent.

So I decided to break it down even further. Now that I had basically provided the information about what to introduce, I realized I could also provide the information about "to whom" an introduction would be helpful. Why burden the person trying to help me? One of my clients sells to compliance officers at financial institutions. Another one sells to project managers in construction. A third does legal contracts for municipalities. Each of these industries and positions are searchable on LinkedIn. It is even possible to identify which of the desired target group is a connection to someone we already know.

So we started to experiment. When asked, "What can I do to support your growing business," the worst thing a CEO can answer is something vague like, "Think of me when a prospect might need me." Rather, I recommend going ahead and doing the work for them. The most important step is researching something great about the prospective client. Then, I send an email that says something like:

> I see that you know __(person)__ at __(company)__ . I am so impressed with how he/she/they _____.
>
> I would love the chance to work with them and think I can help with __(service)__ . Here is a bit more information.
>
> Will you please provide an email introduction for me?
>
> Thanks.

With this formula, we are seeing closer to an 85 percent success rate in obtaining referrals. People want to help, and they love to share compliments. It is our job to break it down and make it easy for them to get started.

Delegation is a sign of trust. I am fortunate that in my career I've had so much opportunity to work with young, smart people, eager to learn and take on more and more challenges. So, I have been able to share and delegate fantastic experiences that perhaps they would not have received in a more corporate environment. Nevertheless, sometimes mistakes are made.

In the haste and pressure of entrepreneurial demands, I have indeed trusted people's abilities and delegated too soon. On one occasion, I was working in Savannah, Georgia. There, jet manufacturer Gulfstream is a top employer and a major funder of my organization. Our brand-new intern posted something on social media that I had delegated. Unfortunately, he misspelled Gulfstream. Ouch! That was embarrassing. Nearly a decade later, I am still very close with this young amazing man. He refers to me as his "Savannah mom." He reminded me last week that he checks Google dozens of times daily before sending emails or social media posts. He does not want to relive that experience.

This personal experience reminds me of a story I once read where a senior executive made a big mistake in a company. Basically, it cost them about $100,000. When he reports to the CEO's office to apologize and thank him for the chance to work there, he says, "Thank you for the years of employment; I understand now why I am being fired."

The CEO responds, "Fired? Are you kidding, I just invested $100,000 in your education. You are not going anywhere!"

The most important advice I have here is the observation that the more senior a leader is and the faster that person runs, the *slower* their support staff should go. Too often a high-paced executive encourages rushed behavior around him or her. However, excellent support and delegation is more likely to happen when slow, methodical people are working around and for the rushed, pressure-packed executive. The supporting employees need to be the ones mitigating risks, checking things twice, providing research and supplemental details for conversations, and so on.

I served as the co-president of the High Tech and New Media Club. We were the hosts of the marvelous Cyberposium conference where Guy Kawasaki of Garage.com was our keynote speaker. There were so many moving parts with sponsors, attendees, volunteers, speakers, and more to the conference, there was no way any one person could manage all the details or even have the knowledge to speak about it eloquently. Our team was beautifully organized by the conference chairs, and each area was delegated to capable individuals. Yet that was only half of the solution. The remaining part was how those who made things happen diligently circled back the information and details. Thus, leadership was properly informed and could easily answer questions as necessary to the administration, security, or media.

Chapter 12

Margin, Which Is a Fancy Way of Saying "Grace Under Pressure"

My failed marriage left me as the sole provider and only caretaker for three very young children. Additionally, due to the real estate crash, a costly illness, and an expensive divorce, I was staring down over $700,000 of personal debt. It was devastating.

I didn't actually understand how intense and stressful that time was until I looked back on it. Many years later, as I sat by the pool chit-chatting on a call with a real estate agent, my son's friend walked over and asked me about a sleepover. My son leapt out of the pool, ran over, and screamed, "Don't bother her! She's on the phone!"

Yikes! Obviously, all those years of working three full-time jobs (often being on two conference calls at one time...

thanks speakerphone and mute) had clearly not gone unnoticed and had even taken their toll on the kids. As I mentioned in chapter 4, the most important weapon in my arsenal was a positive attitude. Additionally, I picked up some handy little efficiency tricks along the way. So I want to share some of my favorite ones with you now.

No, this is not a chapter about how to live a crazy life. I pray you never have to do that. I believe some people perhaps take efficiency too far. For example, I once spent a week with a very senior, focused, and driven woman. We attended an intense seminar. I had my six-month-old in tow since he was still nursing. Fortunately, my mother-in-law was willing to join me so I could attend the sessions freely while she tended to the baby. The intense woman kept asking me about juggling my career with parenting. As she did, she sort of stared at my baby with fear in her eyes like he was from another planet. This woman was totally stretched by the demands of her job. She told me that for efficiency's sake she only flossed on upper teeth on even days and did the lower teeth on odd days. Additionally, she never used the microwave for prescribed times like one minute and forty-five seconds because that would involve too many different buttons. She was committed to cooking things for 1:11 or 2:22 or 3:33. Fortunately, the woman eventually married the boyfriend who so patiently waited for her career to settle, and they now have two beautiful children. I like to think that my "alien" baby paved the way.

Nevertheless, she and I did not become best friends. My moderate-paced South Carolina island living was no attraction to her way of life. In fact, I tend to engage the kind of friend who advised me to eliminate this chapter entirely, saying, "In the absence of valuing balance and relationships, you might just help people become more efficient at ruining their kids."

He was kidding, and so am I when I say, "Read on at your own risk!"

All kidding aside, here's a quick note to assure you we never ruin our kids. We love them. We encourage them. We coach, teach, feed, dress, and hug them. I am not a perfect parent, and I am pretty sure you aren't either. Yet, I tell my kids that I am the best mom they ever had. I have learned that the more we relax and enjoy our children, the more they tend to enjoy life and are even motivated to build a life they can appreciate fully. Also, I have noticed the less I stress out about my children, the more confidence they have. They see the trust I have in them. So please give yourself a high-five on a job well done!

Now, back to sharing a trick or two to lighten your load. Timed email is an absolute favorite trick of mine. There are many technological options that can be licensed monthly, and I think timed email is even now a free feature in Gmail and Outlook. Timed email is simply responding to or writing email now but scheduling it to send later. I use this trick in three different ways.

Have you ever felt rushed to start your day? Have you been overburdened thinking you are behind even before you get started? I have, and I hate that feeling. Such tension, especially early in the day, can hijack the most precious morning moments. So, I decided to start my day feeling "ahead" rather than "behind." Routinely, before I even turn on my computer, my Gmail account has a dozen or more emails sitting in the draft folder that are timed to go out at 8:30 a.m. *Ahhh*...doesn't that feel good?

Misplaced ballet slippers? No problem, we have some time to look for them.

Spilled cereal bowl? No problem. I can take a moment to clean it up.

Handsome husband ready to relax together over a fresh cup of coffee? You betcha!

Timed email is the secret to happy mornings. I am generally at a desk by 8:30 a.m. However, thanks to timed email, even if I did not arrive until closer to 9:30 a.m. I would not be "behind."

The relationship-building content is the best part of these emails. They tend to either be emails of gratitude or outreach. One great way to unwind from the day is to make mental note of some good things that were observed during the day. Converting that list into quick gratitude emails is powerful:

"I noticed sales are up this month, great job!"

"Thanks for going the extra mile with your team this week."

Outreach is also essential. I generally have categories of people with whom I need to connect: authors, ghostwriters, speakers, conference organizers, and others. I have served clients whose lists are very different: supply chain managers, construction project managers, buyers, and the like. Additionally, a group could be defined as business contacts in a certain geography. It doesn't matter. When I am expanding my relationship sphere and choose to do so with one type of contact at a time, then I can send a largely repeatable message. Therefore, I will spend a decent amount of focused energy perfecting my message to authors, for example. Once that is done, the rest is largely cut and paste. That part I can do while relaxing nightly to reruns of *The Office*. Cutting and pasting ten emails to be sent tomorrow morning is an easy one-episode task. In some ways it is more relaxing and fulfilling than a glass of wine...and fewer calories!

Before addressing the second and third ways timed email is a godsend, let's pause to emphasize why emails of gratitude and outreach are so mighty. I wouldn't be an MBA worth my salt without mention of a two-by-two matrix at some point. The BCG (Boston Consulting Group) Matrix of market share and market growth infiltrated our lexicons, allowing each of us students to freely (even ad nauseum) refer to terms like cash cow, dogs, and stars.

Heated political discussions with my children have taught me that a two-by-two matrix is the best way to define Democrats, Republicans, Socialists, and Libertarians. I once even relied on the trusty two-by-two-matrix formula to discuss premarital sex with my then-boyfriend, now husband. (Sorry, friend, you'll have to wait for the next book for a full explanation here.)

Perhaps the most famous two-by-two matrix is the Urgent/ Important Matrix popularized by US President Eisenhower.

We don't have to be rocket scientists to recognize that Quadrant I demands our attention. The lesson here is that too many of us spend time in Quadrant III doing what is urgent but not important. Please go ahead, grab a pen (red is best), and draw yourself an upward diagonal arrow from Quadrant III to Quadrant II. The timed gratitude and outreach emails described previously are exactly the important, but not urgent communications that too often get overlooked. Thus, timing my email moves me from Quadrant III to Quadrant II, which simultaneously minimizes Quadrant I. Yippee!

Have you ever lost yourself in an email vortex? Many smart people have written about great strategies like turning off notifications, creating folders, and other methods to battle

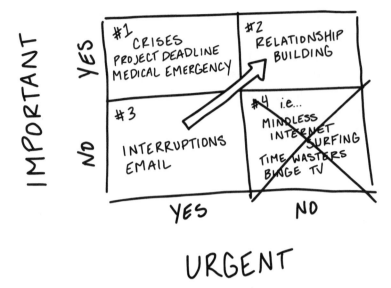

this demon. Please include timed email on your list. The quick reply emails back and forth can be the worst offender fueling the whirlwind. You know what I mean. You sit down thinking you will handle five to ten emails. In stride, you feel great about your answer to the first person. However, before you get on to person two, three, and four, you are sucked into a long string with person number one. Ugh. Unless blood is involved, I recommend never hitting "send now." Sure, you can read and even reply to emails as they come in if you must. Then, I suggest, you make "reply in one hour" your best friend. This simple option will allow you to effortlessly reply to persons two, three, four, and so on before the first has a chance to divert you off course. Magic.

I invite you to consider magnifying the results of this trick by expanding the use with your team. Customer service teams are especially in need of the one-hour buffer. Very few clients are so demanding that they need a response in less than an hour. This delayed-response technique significantly decreases stress on customer service teams by allowing them to make more clients satisfied.

My final deployment of the timed-email trick is a self-made, thus customizable, drip campaign. When I reach out to someone like a potential business partner or prospect, I find it helpful to invest some time in them beforehand. So, I will visit their website, LinkedIn profiles, Twitter pages, and the like. Once I do all that, I want to leverage that time beyond just one email. So I will send three. The first one can be timed for tomorrow morning. The "followup" (news flash—not everyone replies to first attempts) can be timed for next week. And the final effort can be timed for two weeks out. Timing the emails in this way allows me to refer to something unique and wonderful about them while the research is fresh. It also eliminates me having to remember when to follow up. Word to the wise—whenever someone does indeed reply to the first or second email, I have to remember to delete the on-deck subsequent emails from the drafts box.

Automated calendar function is another favorite of mine. Many studies that show the more control you give other people in their day or their job, the happier they are. So an automated calendar has two purposes. One is to put an end to useless time-consuming conversations like, "Are you available on Tuesday at 1:00 or at 4:00 p.m.?" Not only can the tool schedule the meeting, it can reschedule the meeting as needed! Additionally, when I say, "My calendar link is below, grab a time that works for you" people get the control they desire.

This last point is again relevant for customer service teams. Potentially disgruntled clients get a boost in positivity just knowing that their customer service representative is available for them. The client gets control to jump on the calendar as needed. Amazingly, the client demands less of the employee's time while becoming more satisfied.

Some final technology-based time-saving tricks involve conference calls. I spend much of my day on phone calls and prefer to use one conference line. The phone number and code are in the automatic calendaring system so they get included in the calendar invite for me and my phone partner(s). Thus, we waste no time discussing phone numbers or who is calling whom. Second, I never have to look up numbers or remember details, it is all right there. Lastly, it is the same number all day, so it keeps me on track. I often have back-to-back calls with only about a five-minute cushion. I know it is awkward to hear the beep in of the next caller if I have allowed the first one to drag on. So I don't.

More importantly, using a conference line allows for the option of recording the call—this needs permission, of course. If the call is recorded, it frees me up to worry less about note taking, allowing me to either follow along on various web sites or even take a stroll. At one point, I recognized a certain rhythm to my calls. The majority of the first twenty minutes I was scurrying around on the internet to follow the information being conveyed to me. I was also feverishly making note of the most critical aspects of their situation. I generally have the call on speaker phone, freeing up my hands to type. By contrast, in the latter half of the call, I tended to be answering numerous predictable questions. So, at this point in the call, my hands were generally free. One day, my cell phone was sitting next to my desk phone, and I realized I could use it to call in as an additional party to the conference line without disrupting any of the fascinating discussion. Before long, I was still attentive to my conversation, busily answering dozens of questions. Yet this time I was doing so while I was strolling the beautiful city around me and soaking in the gorgeous weather. Back at the office, my desk was empty, but my voice was recognizable through the glass wall that overlooked the hallway. My colleagues started wondering about "the ghost of Bea!"

Since that day, recorded calls and walking and talking are a staple to my conference call life. I now even try to schedule them that way, inviting my call partner to do the same. I explain that I am happy to record the call for free and share the MP3 so neither of us have to worry about note taking. Additionally, there are machine transcription services as inexpensive as $0.10 per minute, so with a $3 investment I can upload the MP3 and minutes later have written notes easy to add to a database, follow-up email, or whatever else I need. These tools allow me to get my work done while I am taking care of my physical and mental health. Not being chained to a desk, yet productive in my work, also afforded me the flexibility for my close friends or children who need an ear from time to time.

The "while system," doing something while doing something else, is a chief tenet of efficiency. This concept goes back to my days in business school, where I would read my cases on a stationary bike at Shad Gymnasium.

Now, having a busy personal and professional life, I continue the tradition. I have a stationary bike under one of my desks. The other desk is a standing desk with a stepper below. Sitting is the new smoking, so I avoid it when possible and do my best to be on the move, even if at a relaxed pace. A moderate pedal or step while working won't prepare me for the Olympics, but it helps contribute to good energy and decent health.

Additionally, a dumbbell on my desk feeds into the "while system." No, I am not a bodybuilder. I am, however, motivated to maintain some tone in my aging arms. My mother warned me often by attempting to flex one bicep only to flap the drooping skin below, saying, "playing the ol' banjo!"

My friend Mary Nestor is writing a business book about the wisdom of older colleagues. She observes that experienced men are welcome in the boardroom. In fact, venture capitalists commonly seek to invest in teams with some "gray hair." On the other hand, she points out that executive business women past the age of sixty are often discredited. Her book aims to change that. Her wisdom is matched only by her wit as she makes fun of the common struggle of sagging arm flesh. Her book's title is *The Right to Bare Arms*. Our friendship serves as a reminder for me to keep my dumbbell pumping even while I sit at my desk.

But is doing two things at once even possible? I know, I know, I have read the research. Apparently, someone in a white lab coat has decided there is no such thing as multitasking. Evidently our brains don't work on two things at once. Nevertheless, it can be a handy business skill—and one specifically sought after by employers to be able to switch quickly between two or three activities.

For me, I believe there are certain tasks that really require longer times of focus. Writing a chapter in a book, preparing a speech, thinking through a detailed contract or negotiation would be examples. So I am diligent about setting aside long stretches of undivided time for such things. "Long stretches" is the operative word for me. For years, I would give myself an hour for such tasks, and it was futile. By the time I wrapped my head around the essential aspects of what I needed to accomplish, the calendar was serving me up a totally different sort of activity. I experienced a powerful breakthrough when I learned that if I could not give myself four or more hours for such tasks, it was better to schedule no time at all. So, this is not the "while system" described earlier at all. Quite the opposite, it is the focus system. Yet, I afford myself time for such periods of focus because, for other tasks, I am able to do two things at once.

For me, the key is deciding how to pair activities for multi-tasking. The mindless emails described earlier are examples. For instance, I enjoy sweeping or raking while listening to and learning from another motivational speaker. And I have never folded clothes or emptied a dishwasher without simultaneously checking in with an extended family member.

My favorite at-home efficiency is to simply hit a button. Besides while camping, I have never had to do laundry down by a riverbank. Rather, I am part of the privileged group that can turn on a washing machine. And with four athletic people in a house, we do so nearly every day. Before leaving for work most days, I would hit the buttons for clothes washer, clothes dryer, dish washer, and even the Roomba vacuum. The genius is not in getting the load of dishes or clothes cleaned. The real benefit is that there is a clear and specific chore for a child to do when he or she comes in from school. Saying, "Sweetie, empty the dishwasher," or "Can you please fold the clothes," is so much more concise, specific, and thus more likely to be accomplished than "please clean your room" or "straighten up the house."

There you have it, a few proven tips on efficiency, saving time, and using technology workarounds. Yet the most impactful productivity advice I have isn't to cut down our tasks, it is to build up opportunity. Seize the moment. It is at unannounced times that chances come to impart wisdom and offer support to our children. Through my business school education, the best learning happened outside the classroom. So, I urge you to become aware in every moment. My best "writing" is done not when I am sitting down to meet a deadline. My best ideas come when I am on a walk, in the shower, or commuting to work. Capturing and investing profound ideas in one of these moments trumps "saving" hours of time.

Chapter 13

Breaking the Mold on Business Travel

"Does that really move the needle?" is a favorite MBA question. The needle we metaphorically refer to is on the gauge of a speedometer. Will making the proposed change just lead to a different path around the slow city block plodding along? Or will implementing this suggestion shift things into a whole new gear? Picture the onramp of the Autobahn and really letting loose.

Those are the questions. The encouragement, and the lesson, is to think big and think deliberately. My business school did a great job illustrating the power of strategically moving the needle. As students, we pored over hundreds of cases. We examined businesses struggling for decades to shave off costs here or bolster revenue there. The hard work is endless. Alternatively, we learned of other companies employing a bolder and more strategic way of thinking about an issue. Thus, they were able to identify a path demanding less effort but yielding tremendously impressive results. Such paths significantly move the needle!

For example, I have often wondered whether I should make a hundred additional sales calls and cut prices by 5 percent to secure some new clients? Or is it better to expand the business geographically or to add a new product line?

Business travel is one critical place where I want to invite you to break the mold, to think boldly and shrewdly in order to really move the needle. Researching business travel "hacks," I found dozens of neat startups and a long list of ways to save $25 to $200. Yuck! All that work for only $25! Tons of mini steps overwhelm rather than encourage me. It feels like a great deal of effort for very little result.

Certainly, meeting face-to-face is the best way to build rapport, invest in relationships, and establish trust. Thus, in today's global world, travel is essential for establishing productive business partnerships and for effectively negotiating agreements. So let's assume we need to keep travel as a line item in our annual fiscal budgets. Business travel is so predominant that for 2019, global business travel was estimated at nearly $1.3 trillion according to the GBTA (Global Business Travel Association).[2] Nevertheless, where there is financial outlay, there is great opportunity for savings. So, I challenge you to cut travel expenses dramatically, maybe even by 50 percent.

---

2   Clarke, P. (2016). "GBTA Forecasts Global Business Travel Spend to Reach $1.6 Trillion by 2020." https://www.travelpulse.com/news/business-travel/gbta-forecasts-global-business-travel-spend-to-reach-16-trillion-by-2020.html

If we are not going to eliminate business travel, can we turn it on its head? Most business travel is done in reaction to a situation or opportunity (let's call this the "reactionary" model of business travel) rather than as an enterprising investment in a relationship (let's call this the "planned" model of business travel). The latter is more productive and way more cost effective. Perhaps envision scheduling relationship-building meetings with ten prospects rather than one contract negotiation meeting with only a specific client.

"Business travel is convenient, inexpensive, and hassle free," said no one...ever. I travelled often and spent significant time building relationships with clients, referral sources, and strategic partners. However, I had small children and even smaller budgets, so impromptu travel was not an option for me. Business travel that catered to one or only a few clients was expensive and particularly disruptive to my family.

So, I took the bull by the horns. Each year I would proactively design visits to four or five cities and decide to spend an entire week there. I selected locations based on the number of large company prospects, law firm referral partners, relevant conferences, and so on. I also wanted to have fun and enriching experiences for my family, so cities where we knew loved ones were strongly considered.

In any given week, I would set up twenty or more appointments or attend an event and make more than fifty meaningful connections face-to-face. These relationships were essential to my budding business, and I maintain many, even thirty years later. But that is not all. In order to make twenty appointments, I often had to reach out to one hundred people with a note saying something like, "I will be in your area on these days, can we set up a time to connect?" If I were coming to town according to the old, common model (in reaction to a specific need of one client or prospect), these one hundred people would never have been contacted. I wouldn't have the flexibility in my schedule to reach out or to meet them. More eminently, it might have seemed disrespectful of their time to contact them on short notice. However, the outreach note to one hundred or so contacts gave them a chance to remember our company, triggered a potential need for our services, and gave me a chance to brag about our latest accomplishments. Of these, generally another twenty would set up a phone call for the week prior to or after my trip in lieu of a face-to-face. The call was much more meaningful than a cold-call sales attempt would have been. Just me mentioning a trip to their area upgraded me from being an annoying salesperson and distraction to being a friendly associate.

I remember early on feeling a bit like a fibber because I would say, "I will be in your area on x day...," when in reality, if the first two or three people responded with "Sorry, I will be out that week, but could meet the week after," I would book my travel accordingly. It only took one "anchor" conference, sales call, partner luncheon, speaking engagement, what have you, then the trip was built around that stake in the sand. The results are undeniable. I almost never flew to meet a client because they had an urgent need for my services or a problem. I found that if I had connected with them within the past twelve months, they were twice as likely to sign up as a client when their need arose. Further, when problems did emerge, we could work through them over the phone because I had built the rapport earlier in person.

I just shared a bit about how I maximized travel budgets and business appointments. But how can it actually be done well for business while balancing family obligations? When I had to leave my young children, it was always somewhat difficult but usually manageable. Nevertheless, I found that a few things helped. I loved involving them by reading about the places I was going and finding them on a map. My favorite trick when I had young readers was to buy two of the exact same book. At bedtime, I would read aloud in the hotel while my child back at home would follow along.

Many people keep business and family totally separate. If that works for you, great! I am the opposite. As teenagers, my kids advise my business, as pre-teens they learned from my experiences, and as young children they often tagged along... and this tagging along even included much of my travel.

Summer is especially conducive for business/family travel combined. We traveled often during the summer for three reasons. First, summer day camps were widely available. Second, business contacts tended not to be crazed with crammed schedules in the summer, so if they were in town, they were more open to a relaxed introductory meeting. Finally, our home was more attractive for house swapping during the summer...more on that in a hot minute.

Right now, let's take a break to talk about the importance of diversity and how it relates to travel. As I have described repeatedly, everything about my business school education is about learning from the experiences of others. Thus, the more heterogeneous the other students, teachers, and case protagonists are, the more fulfilling the education. Therefore, top universities and business schools work diligently to build a class that matriculates from more than a dozen different industries, ranging from consumer products to military, heavy manufacturing, and healthcare. The current HBS student population is roughly 42 percent female, 28 percent ethnic minorities, and 34 percent international. Reportedly, the class of 2016 had representation from seventy-three countries.[3]

This commitment to diversity has certainly enriched me with a supreme variety of perspectives. Some changed my way of thinking altogether. Others have taught me to at least question my bias. All have trained me to surround myself personally and professionally with individuals who will not naturally be inclined to make the same assumptions I might. My dad loved to reiterate the well-used phrase, "Don't assume, or you will make an *ASS* out of *U* and *ME*."

A varied perspective also enriches conversation, cuisine, humor, and more. One of my favorite funny stories comes from my classmate Anjali. She grew up in Brooklyn but often visited India to see extended family. Anjali made an observation about eating grapes in both places. As a young child, she recognized that, in Brooklyn, the grapes grew a thin skin around them, whereas in India, when she ate grapes they were without skin—more squishy and moist. Her Brooklyn home was comfortable, but there were no helpers standing by. In India however, there were many types of personal servitude. Initially, Anjali wondered why grapes grew differently in India than they did in the US. It took years for her to realize the grapes grew the same—the difference was that someone was in the kitchen in India peeling the grapes for her enjoyment.

Joining me on my business travels provided lessons in diversity for all three of my children. They have attended Christian camps in South Carolina, Georgia, and Virginia and camps at Jewish community centers in Savannah, Boston,

---

3   The Albert Team (2020). "What to Know for Harvard Business School: GMAT Scores and GPA." https://www.albert.io/blog/harvard-business-school-gmat-scores-and-gpa/

and San Francisco. They have attended art, sports, wild-life, technology, and dance camps and have made friends in dozens of divergent cultures and locations. I would love to tell you that I am the thoughtful mom that sits down with inter-esting options for my child and allows him or her to choose how they will spend their days based on their passions and interests. Nope. I cared about safety for them, affordability for us, and convenience for our schedule. We did whatever was necessary to make the week productive for work and still let me be "home" to hear about their days, have dinner, and put them to bed.

Of course, we didn't always have summer day camps as an option. So I have some tricks for year-round travel, too. First of all, I never minded taking pre-high-school kids out of school. As a kid, I missed school constantly. My mother loved to take me out not only for doctor's appointments, but even for life experiences. She was phenomenal about taking advantage of our surroundings. We never knew how long we would live in any one area of the country, so she made sure we experi-enced that area while we could. Living in California, we were sure to visit Yosemite. Living near New York City, she worked out dinners in Chinatown and had us stand in the two-for-one ticket line for Broadway shows. Bureaucratic requirements on school attendance were not going to stand in her way. On the rare occasion that my dad finally got some vacation time, my gracious southern mother argued with the principal: "Like hell we're going to stay in town for school!"

Late spring each year, I remember her calling the atten-dance office to inquire how many days I had missed for that year and how many more could I afford before risking being held back a grade. If two remained, she would arrange a museum day. Boy, was she mad when she learned that I had left a Social Studies project to the last minute. We were all to spend the day at the Metropolitan Museum of Art, so into the car we climbed. However, I had to complete a diorama due early the next morning. So, I schlepped my shoebox and bag of artifacts, glue, markers, and everything around the city. While my family explored inside the museum, I sat outside in the sun on those iconic steps cutting and pasting. I must have gotten focused on my figurines and the details I was creating as I temporarily forgot how embarrassing it was to be a teenager doing homework outside. When I finally looked up, I realized that a crowd had gathered around me to take note of my "art," thinking I was some sort of child prodigy. "Why else would she be outside on the steps of the world's number one museum?" they must have thought....

I suppose the legend of the apple not falling far from the tree has me here. I share my mother's vision that, especially in the early years, some schoolwork can be made up later, and that enriching family time is priceless. So, it was not unheard of for me to organize one or two trips during the school year. In these times when summer camps were not an option, my business travel entourage included not only a husband and three kids, but also a doting grandparent or two. While I was at my sales calls, conferences, or speeches, their Oma would take children to the zoo, a historical site, or an art museum. I am so blessed to have had that help.

I can hear you wondering through the pages, "How on earth did you afford the hotel bill?" Confession: I am a house swap addict. I have now taken my children to dozens of places and stayed for "free" in Chicago, New York, San Francisco, Atlanta, Washington, DC, Vail, Breckenridge, Boone, and even a month in Austria. In total, hotel stays for all of the repeated trips we have enjoyed would have cost well over $200,000.

How does it work? For roughly $200 a year, I create a profile of our home complete with pictures and descriptions. I have had equal success on both www.homeforexchange.com and www.homeexchange.com. Any of the sites seem to let you search your desired locations for free. I recommend searching all the sites and determining which one has the best options for homes in locations where you want to travel. Then set up an account on that site.

I am so often asked about this house swap addiction of mine that I wanted to lay out not only the "what" but the "how" as described above. Additionally, I will go one level deeper and answer the four most common questions:

1. What was your best experience?

We were going to a ski resort in Colorado and swapping with our home on the coast in South Carolina. In one conversation with my swap partner, I reminded her, "Please remember that although our dog will be at the kennel, a yellow Lab does live here, so if any of you are allergic, this is not the place for you." She responded by telling me how much she loves dogs, especially Labradors and how much they will miss their dog while they are on vacation. She even asked if I would *mind* if they kept our dog at our home! The result: $300 savings and happier dog!

She later phoned me to ask, "Will you be renting a car from the Denver airport?" That was my intention, until she continued that, "Parking at the airport is expensive, would you mind driving our car for the week?" Another $300 savings. As we became friends, I realized she was general counsel for a large telecommunications company who licensed a great deal of software. You guessed it. She even became a client. Cha-ching!

2. What was your worst experience?

One time we arrived (two parents, three children, and two grandparents for eight days for a week of work in DC). The neighborhood was great, and the home was huge, as advertised. Yet, the owner had been travelling for a while and had apparently not communicated with his son that the house was to be left clean. It was unacceptable, down to the SpaghettiOs still in the pan on the stove. Upon arrival, I did my typical walk-through, but did not let anyone else even get out of the car. For a moment, I was livid at the thought of paying for numerous hotel rooms for more than a week. Then I called a maid service and paid $300 for them to clean every surface, change sheets, everything. Interestingly, I never even bothered to tell my house swap partner. At first, I didn't want to ruffle a feather while he was at my home. Later, after staying eight days with seven people (which would have cost me $10,000 in a nearby hotel), I did not care at all about the cleaning charge.

3. What is your favorite part about house swapping?

Raising my kids as 'house swappers' has certainly shaped them. They experienced New York City not in the high-speed elevator of the Hilton but by riding another child's scooter through Central Park. My favorite story is when my island-raised seven-year-old was playing outside our Chicago house swap. He had a Wiffle Ball bat and formed a pick-up game with the neighborhood kids in the playground. This mini green oasis was surrounded by apartment homes, so wildlife was pretty much restricted to squirrels and bugs. The ball went into a small bush. Before retrieving it, my son banged the bat on the ground as he back home was trained to do in order to alert any unwanted critters. His new city friend asked, "What is he doing?"

My answer only made his eyes wider: "Scaring away the snakes."

4. What surprised you in the process?

Every time, before we left for a house swap, I set out three large bins, one for each child. I explained that they could put away any toys, books, stuffed animals, and anything else that they did not want to have a stranger touching. I said that, in this case, it was okay to not want to share. We would store it safely up in the attic until our return. Never did any of my children put an item in the bin. Rather, they asked, "Remind me who is coming to our home?"

"A six-year-old girl and a four-year-old boy," might be my reply. As our departure neared, I would hear them strategize as they left out certain items: "I think he would enjoy this book," or "I hope she likes my painting easel."

House swapping isn't for everyone. Neither is schlepping kids around on business travel. Those were my personal preferences born from a drive to enrich my family's experiences. Surprisingly, following that inclination for my family actually led to me cutting my business travel budget significantly. When I changed the model from reactionary to planned, the needle really moved, in terms of what I could accomplish on the road and how little money I would have to spend doing so.

Part 4

Go Forth and Prosper!

- **You've Got the Tools, So What's Your Vision?** •

- **Circle the Wagons** •

- **Write Your Ticket: Because You Can!** •

- **Lagniappe: A Little Bit Extra, for You** •
  and Those Around You

ACROSS:
1. SHAPE
2. SMALL

DOWN:
3. DO THIS WITH A PEN
4. MORE

Chapter 14

You've Got the Tools, So What's Your Vision?

"Culture eats strategy for breakfast" is a famous quote by Peter Drucker and sums up why this book is predominantly about things like authenticity, resilience, curiosity, and kindness. These and other qualities build fertile cultures, so they deserve the bulk of our attention. Nevertheless, in chapter 13 we whetted our appetites for strategy's power by examining how a specific blueprint on one small area like travel can have a big impact. So, although culture has earned its place dominating this book, chapter 14 is dedicated to your vision: defining, declaring, and disseminating it!

What is your plan of action? For your business? For your family? For your life? Before we dive into answering these questions, let's explore why it is important to do so.

Months after I laboriously earned my MBA with Distinction from Harvard Business School, we moved to Munich. I mentioned these plans to everyone I met, and 90 percent of the time I was asked the exact same question. "What sort of work does your husband do that takes you overseas?"

"My husband?" I thought. I didn't even mention that I was married. They had concluded things about my family based on their own perceptions, not my story.

Decades later, when I told people I would be travelling through Australia with my children, dozens of people said, "You are so lucky. I wish I had money to do that!" Again, their statements claiming to be about me in effect had no relevance to my life, nor did they reflect our truth of a frugal trip afforded from vacating a permanent residence.

We don't live in isolation. The world is often assuming, stating, and misstating your reality. As I write this, I can see my friends of different races and sexual preferences nodding in agreement yet tisking while saying, "Girl, you don't even know!" I appreciate the underscore. If we don't define ourselves, our situations, our goals for ourselves, someone will do it for us.

Sometimes, like my examples above, it is harmless. What someone else thinks of me, my husband's work, or my travel plans, is truly none of my business. Nevertheless, other times, inaccurate perceptions can hurt. They can stand in our way or they can mitigate potential aid. "Separated" is a label I owned for nearly a decade. As a result, I wore a cloak of society's erroneous assumptions about my hopes, intentions, financial stability, and personal safety, all of which closed doors of needed assistance for me and my family.

I was judged, often wrongly and definitely unfairly. You will be too. I am not inviting you to cry. I am crying out for you to invite. Invite help, encouragement, support. State your deepest dreams, hopes, plans, and ideas to yourself. Then girdle yourself with friends, supporters, and a team who will get you there.

Let me be clear. Even your most loving friends will bring you down unintentionally if you let them. They care about you, so they will ask how you are doing. You share your concerns and problems with them, so naturally they are going to follow up and ask about those. But remember, your energy is fertilizer. Whatever receives your vigor will grow. Choose wisely.

I have found that not every question calls for a detailed answer. "Whatever happened with your child getting in trouble at school?" and "How did it end up with that disgruntled employee?" are in fact the same statement. They are saying, "I listen to you. I care about you. I want to help." From here, the choice is ours. We can respond by spending the next hour rehashing the minutiae around a situation that has already been resolved. Doing so is likely to stir up negative emotions, drain our vitality, and steal away a beautiful opportunity for growth.

Alternatively, we can open up space for this caring supporter to feed into one of our deepest desires. No mention of the trouble at school is required. It is perfectly acceptable to answer, "He is doing much better, thanks. He has taken an interest in playing the drums, do you have any recommendations for teachers or music shops?"

So, where are you going? In your life? In your family? In your work? Articulating our master plan is always challenging. This is in part because we can set our intentions, yet we are not fully in control. Nevertheless, we must establish a game plan in order to give ourselves the greatest chance for success.

There are four times when an accepted clear course of action is especially important to describe. Paths that are particularly unique, making a major change, involve many people, or require moving at a rapid pace will call for stellar vision setting.

Innovation, by definition, is challenging the norm. So, when we are bringing a drastically new perspective, we must make sure everyone is on the same page. Two of my favorite pictures are of innovative perspectives my children offered. In one, they have moved the bunk bed railing to the floor and are using it as a tennis net. In the other, my son has flipped a mini plastic slide and is "running" on it like it is a treadmill. I have found that thinking outside of the box is an incredible recipe for success. Additionally, I recognize that the ability to think outside of the box is sometimes inversely correlated with one's ability to express that unique perspective. This is because the best out of the box thinkers are those that don't see the box in the first place. Thus, they might not recognize the need to articulate the gap between typical assumptions and the inventive viewpoint. If this is you, pat yourself on the back for your imaginative mindset, but be sure to check in often with those around you.

Carolin Archibald, past president of Medela, was a classmate of mine and is a dear friend. So, I am blessed to watch and learn from her intentional management approach. One thing that strikes me, even in casual conversation, is how thorough Carolin is in communicating where we are and where we are headed. She doesn't skim the details with a quick invitation, "How about a hike today?" Rather, she is more likely to present a detailed option, saying something like, "It is a beautiful day! I was thinking we could do the low-impact five-mile ring today. If we leave by ten in the morning and pack a lunch, we can enjoy the best views and still be back in time to make dinner. How does that sound?"

Similarly, a public speaker acquaintance of mine enjoys huge success. He is sought after, commands a high fee, and even sells his products successfully from the back of the room. Yet, to me, his talks seem sort of slow and even repetitive. One time, he shared a vignette and described the main character by saying, "She makes soap; you know, the stuff we use to clean our bodies."

I thought, "Did he really just explain soap?" I tell you this story, not to pick on him, but to pick on me. My pal didn't literally think a definition was imperative. Rather, he was using the phrase as a built-in pause, sort of a breather, to allow any straggling listeners to catch up. Personally, I need to learn to slow down, to let audiences know where we are heading, to ensure that everyone stays with me, and to bring the crowd to the final destination. What about you? Do you tend to be more meticulous or random when conveying a discovery?

The second area which demands alignment of understanding is where there is potential for a major pivot. Studying business in 1998 and 1999 was particularly interesting given the internet boom. Dozens of new cases were hot off the presses for us to analyze to what degree a company should reconsider their brick-and-mortar versus online investment, market share, and revenue expectations.

We were also fortunate to learn directly from business icon Clay Christensen, best known for the book he had just published in 1997, *The Innovator's Dilemma*. Christensen's work epitomizes the importance of the two points just discussed: innovation and pivots. He introduced the concept of disruptive innovation. As a Ford girl, I delight that the Model T is one illustration of disruptive innovation. The innovation was not the luxury automobile available only to a few buyers. Disruptive innovation occurred when the assembly line made the Model T so affordable that it displaced horse-drawn carriages.

Can you imagine what it would be like to reveal such a drastic new way of thinking? Are you, by chance, hiding away a breakthrough idea because other people don't share your ability to see its promise?

Finally, the greater the number of people you lead and the faster the pace of your work, the clearer the picture you must paint for your organization.

Many companies are excellent at conveying plans of action through custom-designed wall posters hanging all through the offices. Employees and visitors are consistently facing the CEO's visuals for where the company is headed and goals individual employees are achieving. Charts display client and revenue targets. Key performance indicators and their success rates are exhibited with color-coded schemes. This can be incredibly powerful, especially when done in an encouraging and positive manner and *only* when the outward appearances match the inward integrity.

You and I have got to do the same thing at work and at home. Let's be masters at articulating and communicating our intentions. Don't keep your blueprint a secret. Let others in on it so that they can carry the burden with you and share in the excitement of getting to the finish line.

I have a vision board that adorns the wall above my desk. It is gorgeous and says things like:

Pay for Savannah, Robert, and William to attend college
Travel to South America

Publish the book, *What an MBA Taught Me...But My Kids Made Me Learn.*

Does such a board work? Well, lots of things and people certainly helped along the way, so it is not like the board jumped off the wall and put his book in your hands. On the other hand, looking at the lovely reminder was and is motivating.

My board was a gift from an employer. In this company, every employee was invited to complete a survey about personal and professional goals, favorite hobbies, preferred color schemes, and so on. Then, a graphic designer was hired to create individual and aesthetically pleasing wall decorations that connect people with each other as well as their own dreams.

Vision boards should *not* be far-fetched, to-do wish lists that are never or rarely achieved. They are best when seen as action plans. They can be beautiful but should not be permanent. Be willing to change, upgrade, and enhance yours. And don't reserve all the forecasting just to the board. I post encouragement on walls and mirrors. Spring clips hang on our kitchen cabinets broadcasting laminated strips filled with proclamations of our future. My home is more likely to have a wall hanging about a hug or family love than it is financial, community service, or sports goals. However, I have a friend who has all these things and more written out on family placemats. They deliberately communicate the family strategy daily.

Deciding on a course of action is one thing. Putting it into place and then tracking progress are two other challenges altogether. Although the popular business tool Balanced Scorecard (BSC) system is renowned for the latter, it was my son's basketball that informed the former for me in a meaningful way.

Every indicator pointed to our company's need to organize around vertical markets like financial services, healthcare, and manufacturing, so the game plan was set to do so. Nevertheless, there remained great trepidation about how to transition company leaders in specific disciplines like marketing, sales, or operations into mini-CEOs of newly formed divisions. What happens when these executives take the risk of embracing their new roles, but they fall short? What if they make mistakes as they transition and learn?

These questions rolled over and over in my head as I sat in the bleachers watching Robert's basketball game. He had been connected to this team for three years, and I was amazed to see how much two of his teammates had improved, especially with their three-point shot. Robert did his thing on offense. He got into position, grabbed the rebound, and put the ball up for two points: Mr. Dependable! He was like an insurance policy for the team. His work under the boards couldn't guarantee that his teammates would sink their three-pointers. Yet, because of his rebounding, their low-percentage outside shot rarely resulted in a turnover. So his stability enabled them to take risks.

Then it hit me; in our company, Julie was Robert. Julie was our one executive who had experience in marketing, sales, and operations. She was versatile and dependable. So the others would be able to take some risks and still have a teammate who could minimize the downside. Thus, we could transition to our newly proclaimed vertical market plan with confidence. Moving the sales leader to head up a division dedicated to serving only manufacturing clients, we could expect sales to be phenomenal there, whereas they might need some help with operational efficiencies or marketing, for example. Similarly, when our head of corporate marketing was promoted to the mini-CEO of the financial services vertical, there would be voids.

I commended Julie for her breadth of expertise and even shared how her ability to stand in the gap so others could take risks and grow was parallel to rebounds on a court. Immediately, she understood. We were able to execute effectively in this new powerful strategy.

But how do I really know? That is where the balanced scorecard comes in. Balanced scorecards are a cornerstone of business school education which teaches that the four perspectives of the BSC are financial, customer, internal process, and learning and growth. The objectives for each are identified and described in detail. Then, key performance indicators (KPIs) are established and connected to each role in the organization.

I prefer KPIs that are results rather than task oriented. For example, tracking the number of people who have signed up for our mailing list is more helpful than counting the number of social media posts that go out. Similarly, knowing the dollars of sales closed means more than the number of phone calls made.

Mostly, because team coordination is paramount, specific roles should roll up into "parent" priorities. My sales number goal should become a part of the overall goal my manager has. For individual advancement, growth, and learning it can be acceptable to have straggling KPIs that don't feed into a team goal. Yet, 80 percent or more of each individual's contribution should in some way coordinate with the charge of the team. Imagine how dysfunctional it would be to have individual goals working in isolation or even conflict with each other. A well-thought-out BSC can avoid this and point the ship in the right direction.

But how do we stay on course? Posters, milestones, even email reminders might help. Conversation, however, is best. Since I tend to be ADD, I have to be careful with interruptions like random phone calls or drop-in desk visits. I welcome them, because if I didn't, I would be closing off my chance at learning about concerns early on, before they become significant problems.

Yet, pop-in disruption isn't my management style. I prefer regularly scheduled team and individual huddles. The term *huddle* prevails over *meeting* because a check-in is often all that is needed. My dad ran auto assembly plants with nine thousand employees and never had meetings where people sat. He found if they stood, they paid more attention and wasted less time. With direct reports, I recommend a weekly or semi-weekly connection. When done properly, the benefits come before and after, not during that time. The previously clearly established targets do the heavy lifting such that the meeting time emerges as relationship growth. The cadence or rhythm of a consistent pattern creates space for personal growth. The junior person, knowing he or she will be speaking with his or her boss in a few days, can in the meantime write down observations about the business, consider thoughtful improvements, and basically think independently. Then the huddles become a time to direct rather than dictate.

Fifteen-minute team huddles are also crucial, daily if possible. Think about that breakfast time with your kids and how powerful it is for setting a tone for their day. The same can be true at work as long as it doesn't slip into an egotistical trap or micro-controlling mechanism. I have had success with very frequent (sometimes daily), super-fast, non-mandatory team huddles where I can pour into the people working so hard to make my dreams a reality.

Chapter 15

Circle the Wagons

"Circle the wagons," my roommate Tami instructed. We were in our twenties, launching our careers, and setting the foundation for a lifelong friendship. Many nights we stayed up discussing our aspirations until three in the morning. On this particular evening, I had just shared that I was seeing a professional psychotherapist. I went on to explain that I had areas of abuse, regret, obsession, and anxiety from my youth that I didn't want to carry into adulthood. Tami listened intently, offered encouragement, and stated, "Circle the wagons."

I had not been familiar with the phrase, so she went on to explain. Pioneers of the late-1800s western migration faced many dangers. Threats came from Native Americans, bandits, wild animals, and more. Whenever the trail blazers perceived a potential problem, they recognized that the safest way to encounter it was to fortify themselves by placing all of the wagons in a circle. The strongest members of the group would be on the exterior on the lookout while the most vulnerable would be protected inside the ring. Tami continued by observing that, like the explorers, I was entering a long journey, one that would be physically and emotionally trying. She warned that some days would be more difficult than others and that I would need to surround myself with dear friends, and she wanted to be the first to claim that role. Lucky me. Thirty years later and she hasn't shaken the title yet.

Recently, I got together with a twenty-three-year-old friend who was seeking some support as she worked through some family issues. You guessed it! I encouraged her to circle the wagons, and I raised my hand!

Who are your wagons?

For whom are you a protective wagon?

You have gotten this far in a book that is all about people skills. Now, let's take some time figuring out who your people are. Defining your "people" isn't singularly about protection. It is about power, influence, enjoyment, and precious human connection.

Susan Pinker's TED Talk "The Secret to Living Longer May Be Your Social Life" has over two million views. By studying centenarians in an Italian village, she researched the ten top indicators of staying alive. Although some likely-anticipated predictors like clean air and exercise do make the list, the top two are distinctly features of our social life.

Paramount is social integration. These relationships can often be surprisingly superficial bonds like talking with your barista or postman. Pinker claims, "Those daily interactions are the strongest predictors of how long we will live."

My dad has always been able to engage any stranger. I remember during high school working at McDonald's. My coworkers loved for him to come in for the $0.86 pancakes and

$0.14 coffee combination special. He found out more about the cashier during the brief transaction than I did in a full eight-hour shift. Similarly, during his career, my dad made it a priority to learn thousands of names of employees in the Ford Motor Company plant. My mom was in on the action. She was well trained with her role should they be walking around the plant together on a Saturday. Whenever my dad called out something like, "Jim, looking good!" my mom was welcome to walk up so that my dad could introduce her. However, if he did not start a comment with a name but rather something like, "Making progress!" that was a signal that he was uncertain of this person's name. Therefore, Mom was to either inch away or graciously offer her own name with a handshake before my dad would have been expected to do so. I considered confirming the details of this paragraph with them. However, they couldn't be reached. They were apparently busily talking someone's ear off at a Savannah restaurant. No wonder they are happily in their eighties and they are enjoying more than sixty years of marital bliss.

Pinker describes that the second most critical indicator for us living longer lives is the existence of close relationships. These are the sorts of attachments whereby we can call on someone for assistance in seriously tough times. Who would you call should you need a loan? Who will give you a ride to doctors' appointments? Are you currently stepping up to the plate where there is a similar opportunity for someone to lean on you?

My alma mater is impeccable about connecting people and defining wagons. It begins with section mates and classmates, as well as the opportunity to form study groups. Even long after graduation, the career center continues to serve, faculty appreciate and encourage connection, and the alumni stand strong. The HBS alumni database tallies nearly ninety thousand people. The school facilitates relationships through newsletters, very active social media, reunions, and ensuring that the database is searchable by class year, name, industry, location, and more. The community clearly strives to provide inspiration as well as sort of a safety net for one another.

More than twenty years after graduating, the school continues to feed my soul. My HBS Forum is one primary source. Perhaps you are familiar with the Young Presidents' Organization (YPO), after which the HBS forums were modeled. YPO is a global leadership community with over twenty-eight thousand members spanning 135 countries. Everyone in this select crowd is under forty-five years old and has over fifty employees.

Similar CEO or executive roundtables with less stringent entrance specifications include Vistage, Women Presidents' Organization (WPO), and Entrepreneurs' Organization (EO). The abundance of these thriving peer groups and their expansive reach is testimony to the power of human connection in business. In each of these organizations, members are certain to find business growth through enhanced acumen and networking, In fact, a Dun & Bradstreet data study in 2017 touts that Vistage member companies grew an average of 2.2 times faster than average small and midsize US businesses. To me, that is relevant whether the chicken came before the egg or not. For example, did they grow *because* of Vistage? Or did these companies decide to invest their time and money into Vistage because they were committed to growing? Either way, the result is impressive and begs two questions: Do you seek to grow your business? Are you connecting with the right folks to get you there?

Accountability is also a key element for any of these councils. Sometimes that is done through detailed reporting of clear-cut targets. Additionally, monthly check-ins for both personal and professional updates are common.

Thankfully, as close as the bonds are within these bodies, it is worthwhile to note that these systems allow for progress, growth, and learning without emotional baggage. This might be in contrast to what I have witnessed in many small or family-owned businesses. One of my favorite taglines comes from Sierra Nevada Brewing Company, perhaps one of the nation's earliest and most influential microbreweries. It says, "Family owned, operated, and argued over."

So although these networks serve somewhat similar functions, they are each exceptional in their own way and thus worthy of a few specific notes. For more than sixty years, Vistage has been gathering small roundtables of business leaders to meet for instructional workshops as well as intimate peer conversation. Additionally, Vistage chairs engage more deeply with one-on-one mentorship for their members. I am proud to be a Vistage speaker. Interestingly, although I am regularly the hired "expert" bringing the workshop content, I leave much smarter. Through Vistage connections in New York, Sydney, San Diego, Denver, and Charleston, I am more savvy regarding access to capital, DISC (Dominance, Influence, Steadiness, Compliance) profile assessments and application, authority marketing, and even nutrition.

Women Presidents' Organization blows me away. I remember speaking at their annual summit in Orlando, Florida, during their twentieth anniversary year. Generally when I attend an eight-hundred-plus-person conference, I have a bit of a game plan for what sorts of people I might be best served getting to know. Then I will seek out meaningful conversations with those individuals. At WPO, I recall being more enthralled with each person I met. Everyone there ran at least a $2 million company and some were founders of businesses doing more than $25 million in annual revenue. I thought, "Wow, each woman is more and more interesting." Yet they were also so approachable. So I just sat back and struck up a friendship with whomever came my way.

Later that year, I had the privilege of serving on the WPO board of advisors, so I flew to New York for the small annual meeting. That morning, I took a walk around Central Park Reservoir while talking with a friend about my upcoming meeting. "It is such an honor to be in the room. These are the women that broke the glass ceiling for us," I shared. I love learning from their experiences.

For me, the forum is the ideal option for a peer advisory group. Complete with all the wisdom I need as well as a direct tie back to my alma mater. It is the alumni associations in major cities that make forums available. Since I don't live in a major city, I fly to New York monthly for my forum. It might be the best investment I make.

Eight to twelve people are compiled after completing a brief survey, which ensures that each forum has a powerful mosaic as well as lacks any conflicts of interest. Each member is required to attend a brief "training" where certain protocols will be discussed. Confidentiality is of utmost importance. Many customs are standardized in order to facilitate safe and balanced conversation. For example, there are time limits on presentations, questions are encouraged to be open-ended, and feedback should ignite, not extinguish, conversation. All of the dynamics are carefully designed to allow the sharing and learning to go deeper and keep the conversation from getting sidetracked.

As a result, in very short order, my tribe of twelve have bonded into deep friendships. We have supported each other's decisions about whether to start or fold companies, terminate employees, or retire from very senior positions. In addition, we have cried together over divorce, wayward children, and abusive spouses. I think Pinker would approve!

Let's take a look at your personal sphere to whom you provide guidance as well as from whom you receive encouragement and information. In chapter 14 we talked about setting a vision. But for whom? Is it just for your children or your direct reports? Are you merely guiding those directly under your authority? I think not. It is worth examining.

Two parting thoughts of advice regarding your sphere are: 1) Sometimes we need to prune, and 2) sometimes we need to share our fruit.

Kenny Rogers sang it best in "The Gambler" explaining that you have to know when to hold your cards or fold them, and when to walk away or even when to run. Let's face it. Bad relationships are a gamble. Are you still feeding toxic associations in your life?

Worse yet, you might even be attracting new virulent individuals. Don't. Drama is catnip for destructive bonds, so we need to do our best to avoid it. One good antidote to this energy-guzzling behavior is to constantly ask yourself, "Can I express this observation or concern more calmly?" or, "Is my tone, vocabulary, or volume in any way inflammatory?" The look-at-me culture shaped by Facebook and Instagram has primed us for show-off, so we need to be especially intentional, even disciplined, to put an end to these habits.

How do we spot the turbulent type early on? Usually, a little listening can do the trick. An acquaintance recently invited me on an outing. I was looking forward to getting to know her, so I was happy to spend the afternoon hearing what she had to say. I perceived a great deal about her estranged spouse, the one adult child with whom she was not on speaking terms, the other adult child who apparently was making endless critical mistakes in his life, the job from which she was freshly terminated, and the unjust way in which she was treated by a prospective employer. As "Eeyore" went on to describe how "at peace" she was, I felt overcome with tension. No, I don't condone being only a fair-weather friend. Where is the intimacy in that? We do, however, need to be mindful about where we can influence. I noted with care that each of the situations she described was indisputably the other party's fault. I will proceed with caution or consider pruning.

Being someone's wagon is a fulfilling chance to grow. It is also a good way to build the team that will be available to fortify you when the time comes. Do you volunteer? Are you giving to your local community? These are no-lose propositions. In my experience, the time and energy spent is in many ways magnified.

My institution promotes community service first by requesting it in the application process. While on campus, service is fostered through club activity, select case readings, and passionate guest speakers. Alumni are later encouraged to participate in structured mentoring and community service projects. Service tends to open us up to new learning and meaningful relationships.

Some of the most powerful and impressive people I know I have met through the Aspen Institute. They galvanize resources into impact mitigating poverty, enhancing education, revamping healthcare, curbing violence, providing clean water, and so, so much more. Many are wealthy and some are famous. Others are resource strained. Some have endured the most horrific crimes and tragedies. Yet, all fight to make their time on this planet matter.

I am insanely blessed to be connected to Aspen by South Carolina's Liberty Fellowship, which has fed me with countless values-based leadership summits and meaningful relationships. The Fellowship was born out of a concern that South Carolina was number one in everything terrible like unwanted teen pregnancy and number fifty in everything great like education. Selection into the group is less about title, education, and experience. Rather, what matters most is one's community contributions.

The area I care about deeply is job creation and entrepreneurship. Mentoring a local startup or judging a business plan competition is thrilling. Additionally, I connect with women from twenty-four countries through the Millennial Women Network. I hope you will join me there.

My most rewarding and fun community service is not structured at all. It might be creating sidewalk chalk encouragement for nurses or elderly in assisted living. It could be baking cookies for firefighters. The best way I have found to shape the insides of ourselves is to put attention outside of ourselves.

Chapter 16

Write Your Ticket
BECAUSE YOU CAN!

"**C**ongratulations! You'll be able to write your own ticket!" was all I heard when I was first accepted to Harvard's MBA program. In fact, I initially heard this idiom the day I was accepted to Emory University nearly a decade earlier. "Write my own ticket!" I liked the sound of that. It is so freeing, so flexible. I could go anywhere.

I graduated high school in the 1980s in New Jersey. Thus, it is in my blood to be a Bruce Springsteen fan. Scenes from the "Born in the USA" video were shot in my dad's Ford plant as well as my school's parking lot. Do you love our green uniforms? Like many, I prefer the song "Born to Run"! All that energy, freedom, breaking loose, endless possibility. For me, the intense emotions Bruce delivers in a passion-packed performance of "Born to Run" is precisely what I feel when I hear, "You'll be able to write your ticket!"

This privilege to me means more than just a travel destination, it means living life on my own terms, being able to define success personally. Basically, it is a blank check to live a life by design rather than by someone else's demands. So, as I heard the phrase, the last thing I envisioned was a pyramid shape where all the points at the bottom rise only to reach the same landing place. No way! I pictured the opposite. People who could write their own ticket would mushroom out, branch beyond to destinations unimagined. But do they?

Fast-forward to my five-year reunion. For each reunion, a thick book-like program is created to include the schedule for the weekend accompanied by pictures, home addresses, and professional information as well as updates of classmates. This time they also asked for one line of advice. Mine was, "Write your ticket!"

Emory University was the first place I stretched my wings to survey the world's possibilities. Up until college, we all pretty much have to study a set curriculum, and our days are largely structured. But going away to school broke open the gates. I studied art history, comparative US and UK politics, various types of literature, and even double majored. There, I abandoned the desire to achieve or succeed for the sake of doing so. Instead, I was enthralled with the joy of learning. Easy access to Atlanta and the city's cultural treasures presented another exploration frontier.

I wondered how my classmates intended to "write their ticket." Yet when I inquired, I was met with a blank stare. Didn't I know? They were pre-med. "Wasn't everybody?" they seemed to say. Sure, the world needs doctors, but Emory had a gravitational pull shifting more and more people in that direction. It was as if we were all standing on an imaginary first rung of a ladder, the next rung was apparently science prerequisites, then applying to medical school. Anything deviating from that path appeared second-rate.

Briefly, even I dipped my toe into the pre-med vortex. As a psychology major, I needed to take a biology class, and I had the option of doing so with or without a lab. I chose the more intense lab version which was a must for anyone considering medical school. The pressure was intense, which really came to a head on the unit where we dissected a fetal pig. On test day, the lab had dozens of stations, each set up with trays holding a fetal pig or a specific part of the pig. On each tray was a pin attached to an arrow that pointed to a particular muscle, vein, or organ. As we carried our test booklets around, we read questions like, "the blood in this vein is going next to which organ?" or "food in this organ came from where?" The test took forever! Several people at stations in front of me were stopping to call over TAs (teacher's assistants) and ask them questions. I wondered what they were saying because although the test was difficult, it seemed pretty straightforward. Or so I thought until I received my grade. I earned a 13 percent. Amazing, right?

As a result, I learned one of the most important lessons. People cheat. Turns out that students kept calling over TAs so the TA could confirm where the arrow should be pointing. Then, often when the TA wasn't looking, the student would "accidentally" spin the arrow so it would be pointing in the wrong direction while the next student struggled to answer the question. Hmmm. No, I am not saying this was common at my incredible alma mater or even typical of pre-med students. Nevertheless, I learned that this sort of "edge out the other guy" was so expected and understood by many of my classmates.

I am not saying I am more righteous than the next guy. I have plenty of moral flaws. Quite frankly, cheating in boring ol' mandatory high school typing class might be a viable option. But we were in college. We could study anything we wanted. We could pursue our dreams. Why waste your time doing anything that requires cheating?

In business school, the story was less dramatic, but the results were similar, especially at first. Now we were theoretically higher up on the imaginary ladder, but the options seemed to constrict rather than expand. The pat question, "What are you going to do after graduation?" had two seemingly defensible answers, "consulting for McKenzie" or "I-Banking at Goldman Sachs."

Why is it that the more credibility we gain, the more constraints we give ourselves? Happiness expert Shawn Achor, who spent twelve years at Harvard studying and working, observes, "what I found in my research and my teaching is that these students, no matter how happy they were with their original success of getting into the school, two weeks later their brains were focused, not on the privilege of being there, nor on their philosophy or their physics. Their brain was focused on the competition, the workload, the hassles, the stresses, the complaints." I am a huge fan of his book *The Happiness Advantage* and I respect the work of his thriving company GoodThink, Inc. Achor's TED Talk is my all-time favorite. So, I mean no discourtesy when I summarize his work simply, "No one writes the damn ticket!"

Fortunately for me and my classmates, curiosity started to blossom about halfway through our MBA. It was the dawning of the internet boom, after all, so the breaking of norms was the new norm. I served as the co-president of the High Tech and New Media Club, and we had the privilege of hosting various treks around cities like Austin, New York, and San Francisco. Nearly three hundred students spent their own money and gave up their spring break (traditionally a time for major

corporate recruiting) in order to fly to California and participate in the high-tech trek. There they were able to engage in
small informational gatherings with Silicon Valley CEOs. The
McKenzie recruiter that was in such demand only a year prior
was now trying to woo MBA candidates with lobster dinners
and ski weekends.

Were people starting to write their own ticket? Or was it
the case that our community's definition of "desired path"
stretched to include founding a dot-com? I suppose we will
never know. For me, I bypassed McKenzie, Goldman, and dot-
coms and headed for my dream of living in a foreign land and
speaking a different language.

By the time five years had passed, my heart and life were
full. So the one line of advice I would offer was clear: write
your ticket! I want people to ask themselves: What if you took
a road less traveled? What if you did what you wanted to do,
instead of what society automatically applauds and showers
with money? Instead of taking the next right step for your
resume, what if you actually took a moment to ask yourself,
what would be the next right step in your life?

Unfortunately, calling your own shots can be easier said
than done. As depressing as this might be, I think we need to
face the facts that our culture presents real hurdles. There is a
strong tide, and it can be very challenging to swim upstream. I
am speaking about overprogramming. For example, it should
be obvious that the parent is the boss. However, when we live
within the demands of today's culture, this is a challenge.
Three- and four-year-olds playing organized soccer means
that families are scheduling the parents, their work, and
other siblings around teeny individuals. Similarly, obsession
with travel sports often means that family budgets and qual-
ity time also play second fiddle to the need to compete many

states away. Yet the happy medium can be difficult to find. I have had a role in all of these things, so please don't hear my observations as judgments against you or anyone else's parenting choices. To the contrary, I am sharing that I struggle with having my family fit it yet not be consumed. So please give yourself credit when you are able to live life by your own design, not be another's demands.

I want this for you, for me, and for my children.

"Do you miss your daughter?" Was all I heard two summers ago. It was not an inquiry, but rather a rhetorical question from literally everyone I encountered who knew that my seventeen-year-old was travelling through Vietnam, Cambodia, and Thailand for the summer.

I wondered. Should I admit that not only didn't I miss her, I actually felt like I had found her. I knew that high school's junior year is a tough one full of stress. We live in a country where "stars" like Felicity Huffman and Lori Loughlin were among the dozens of parents facing legal charges for bribery and other involvement in admissions scandals. Clearly strain around academic achievement was rampant. Countless, even in our small community, were the stories of Adderall being misused as the academic performance-enhancing drug of choice.

My daughter was not immune to this pressure plague. In many ways she was especially at risk: we were new to town, and she was one of only two students accepted that year as a transfer into this highly ranked public school.

For the first time in her life, she seemed to walk to the beat of someone's drum...and, by the way, that drum was not so musically inclined. In one school year, my daughter managed to take up a new sport and play at the varsity level, make tons of great new friends, hold down a paying job, hold down a volunteer job, babysit, carpool her brothers, help her single mom, take all advanced and AP classes while scoring no less than a B, and visit fifteen colleges across seven states. As soon as one task was complete, it seemed like the list of *must dos* would grow. Yet, it always seemed like nothing was ever enough. By whose definition?

And then suddenly, in an instant, only hours after her last exam, there I found myself. I was waving good-bye through airport security at 6:00 a.m. as she departed on twenty-four hours of air travel to the other side of our planet. The tug on my heart felt more like a weight slipping down the back of my throat, then landing heavily in the pit of my stomach.

Mine is the daughter who embraces sunrise and chases sunsets. She doesn't just consume what is in front of her or even take a picture. Rather, this is the girl who studies tide charts, researches the sun's patterns, and learns animal behavior. This way she can grab the shot of the kangaroo at dawn or reflective tide pools at dusk. So the fact that she planned and saved for this trip for six months doesn't surprise me.

Did I miss her?

Perhaps I should have delivered the expected answer "yes." However, it was more true that I "anti-missed" her. She was back. She was no longer buried in a narrative of unnecessary expectations. Rather, through Facetime and texted photos, I saw her electric smile. She ate scaly fish, mastered a new version of hacky sack under city streetlights with Vietnamese friends, and kayaked under waterfalls. Savannah was overflowing with gratitude.

I was ecstatic to watch as she wrote her own ticket. Savannah was able to shed the compulsive culture so that creative cultural exploration could thrive. In her true fashion, she filled me and her brothers with bright images, new relationships, and expanded intellect. We researched, followed along on maps, and watched relevant movies. This allowed us to connect with her as she climbed among the tunnels that determined the fate of the Vietnam War and traversed Angkor Wat, a full city lost deep in a Cambodian jungle.

And there it is, ladies and gentlemen. The great irony of the whole "forego your ticket fallacy." Initially, we seek to comply with the expectations of the people who surround us. In doing so, we are in essence robbing those same individuals of the benefits which will inevitably flow from us living the life we are designed to live. Thinking about my daughter's experience makes me ponder about business leadership. How often do we set conveyor-belt-like expectations, policies, and procedures and unintentionally eradicate creativity and genius in the process? Well, let's not. We each have a call on our lives and the world needs us to uncover it, embrace it, and live it out to the fullest extent.

What about you? What is your ticket? Are you willing to write it?

Chapter 17

Lagniappe

A LITTLE BIT EXTRA, FOR YOU AND THOSE AROUND YOU

"**L**agniappe" is my favorite word. It looks fun. It sounds fun /ˌlanˈyap/ (even gives a nod to my beloved dogs). It is a New Orleans term meaning to offer just a little bit more, a bonus. Naturally, I have to include a sort of post-final chapter as a little something extra for you. What comes around goes around...so if you want more, start by giving more.

Harvard Business School lives out the principles of lagniappe through its impeccably planned reunions. At our first reunion five years after graduation, I had both young children in a double stroller and uttered to my husband, "Let's walk over for a bit and just check it out" I expected to return in a matter of minutes. However, we did not return for nearly eight hours.

How is it possible that small children could last so long without a parent appropriately armed with an overflowing bag of supplies carefully packed to alleviate innumerable toddler traumas? Lagniappe, that's how. Harvard went above and beyond. They had arranged petting zoos, clowns, balloons, tents, and *stocked* diaper stations. They offered snacks, milk containers, juice boxes, crayons, activity sheets, and everything that a parent could imagine. There was no need to leave. Brilliant! Because of the auxiliary support, people were able to stay longer, connect with more classmates, have more interactions with potential career opportunities, and otherwise get more than expected out of the whole experience. People skills galore in action, not just theory. Wow!

I wonder in what ways you are going the added mile. Who are you surprising today with your supplemental efforts?

There are a few tricks to practicing lagniappe. One is delivering *more*, by promising less. Exceeding expectations creates an upward spiral of positivity, the power is endless. This can be done by conservatively calculating or even overestimating costs and timelines and then working diligently to meet more aggressive goals. Beat the target.

Another way this can be done is through titles. Mistakenly, we often try to exaggerate our positions. By doing so, we inadvertently convey a capability we might not actually have.

I learned this as a student when we hosted the Cyberposium conference. Attendees who came from all over the country were used to attending major events hosted by teams of professionals and supported by enormous budgets. The fact that we boasted big-name speakers camouflaged the reality that Cyberposium was a student-run activity. Some of the guests were incredibly difficult and even discourteous if one of their demands could not be met. I contemplated, "why are these people so entitled?" Each student assisting with the affair had a name tag that said "staff." I realized that this somewhat inflated title allowed for an assumption that they were paid, and thus to some degree they "owed" something to the disagreeable patron. In the dozens of conferences I have hosted since that time, I only allow helpers to wear name tags that say "volunteer." The difference is palpable.

Lastly, lagniappe is all about follow-through. As a tennis player, I know that I can get my feet in place, take my racquet back, and make great ball contact. However, if I don't follow through, the shot is a miss.

The same is accurate in business and parenting, and maybe even book publishing. So, I want to follow through well with you. I want to tell you a few repugnant stories and then I will extend a perhaps surprising offer.

Before I do that, though, I will share a heartwarming story. My job is to be a speaker and an author. I adore this work for many reasons. Mostly, I love speaking because it is a thrill to meet amazing people and to feel the energy in incredible conferences or in world-class corporations. Additionally, I relish the challenge and thrill of thinking through the precise custom content I can deliver in order to connect especially with each distinct audience. Anyone who delights in his or her work is truly blessed. Since this is the case for me, I am among the most fortunate.

Last year my perspective changed. Hold on, it gets better. I was invited to be the keynote speaker for Women in Consumer & Commercial Finance in the stunning setting of Scottsdale, Arizona. The conference organizer, Amy, connected with my general message, so I was hired many months in advance— yay! As the date approached, she shared that the elite gathering which had been 188 executives the year prior was now over 500. Obviously she was delighted with the success. Yet she did not want to lose the intimate vibe of the event. She sought to foster connections amongst the participants. As we got to know each other over the phone, I revealed that I had once faced over $700,000 in personal debt (hope you didn't skip chapter 3 on failure). Amy recognized that this experience gave me special insight and connective tissue to this precise audience. She asked me to share, to show up authentically, to be vulnerable. I agreed.

The morning of my talk arrived. Towering saguaro cacti lined my path to the hotel's conference area as I approached to open the event with my keynote address. I was intimidated, yet I remembered my commitment. All of me...good and bad... showed up onstage.

What followed was something that changed me forever. The flood of emails, note cards, and social media love brought me to tears. Their gratitude poured over me, filling corners of my soul I had not realized were vacant. Strangers thanked me for sharing a message that they needed to hear, and they went on to articulate ways their lives were improving as a result. It was, and still is, true that I love my work. However, that experience upped the ante. I realized that even if I despised this work, I would do it anyway. Someone needs me to.

Please allow me to share one of those notes with you:

> Your presentation had a profound impact on me and I even got emotional a few times. You are doing exactly what you are meant to do in inspiring women to come together and support one another. Unfortunately, us ladies tear each other down where we should be lifting each other up.

"Unfortunately, us ladies tear each other down, where we should be lifting each other up" is worth repeating. Ouch. Her declaration transported me instantly back to my first experience as a sales manager. My star team member, Carolyn, had recently returned from maternity leave when a rude prospect was unnecessarily uncivil. Carolyn was slightly shaken but managed the situation confidently. I asked her how.

"I am a mom now." She went on to explain that although she was caught off-guard to be spoken to in that manner, she had decidedly meaningful responsibilities now and could no longer afford to let anyone set her back.

Have you allowed people to hinder you? Most of us have. The press gravitates towards stories of one ethnic, racial, or gender group of people marginalizing another. Regrettably, this often fuels our energy in useless directions. Nevertheless, these situations are actual and terrible. I am equally dismayed at how individuals within a group (like "us ladies") adopt a zero-sum mentality to justify mistreating the very people we could and should elevate. We think there is only so much good to go around, so we sharpen our elbows to scrape for our portion.

On the flipside, sometimes we allow ourselves to be targets to such harm because our defenses are down. We think, "they are like me," or, "we are one and the same," or, "we are on the same team."

I assume the best in everyone, to a fault. I so see the world through rose-colored glasses that the one time I was mugged, I actually turned around, thinking my assailant was a friend, and went to hug him. Evidently, it scared him, as he ran off and leapt into a white getaway car.

I don't recommend hugging your mugger. And although I can be a bit Pollyannaish, I am here to inform you that not all people have your best interests at heart. Here are the three terrible accounts I agreed to share. First, the most successful nonprofit leader I have witnessed was edged out of her position by a female board member. The board member was disgruntled by the executive director's audacity to secure an office location that was optimal for the mission of the organization, her employer. In other words, she did her job. However, she did not select the location which would have increased the value of that board member's real estate investment across town. Uh oh. In this situation (as well as others I have witnessed), the executive naively overestimated the loyalty of the board member, assuming she "had her back." Additionally, she mistakenly attributed integrity to the board member and never considered the potential abuse of power connected to the personal financial gain and conflict of interest.

Secondly, a small-town art museum garnered national accolades largely due to a decade of hard work by one outstanding female curator. Board members noticed her achievements and requested that the CEO recognize the team member in some way. The opposite transpired. The female CEO (who ironically often publicly spoke of leveling the playing field and fighting for more rights for women) terminated the star teammate. There seemed to be only so much shine available to women in that environment. Tragically, the CEO feared that the brilliance of the subordinate would eclipse her own glow.

Unethical people come in all shapes and sizes. I am simply suggesting that we remember that often support doesn't come where we might expect.

Finally, a friend of mine was sitting at the parent orientation for a major university. One mom raised her hand and asked this question, "How do I help my kid beat out the others?" Really?

This comment gets to the crux of my surprise offer. If you in any way see this book as a tool for beating out another, taking someone down, or stomping on dreams, then you and I have misunderstood each other. In that case, I sincerely ask that you send me a quick message through our website or social media and let me know that for you, winning is about someone else losing. I will gladly refund you the cost of the book.

Don't get me wrong, I am very competitive, and I hope you are too! As a tennis player, I hate to lose, but love to be beaten. Do you grasp the difference? Being on a court, playing my best and still not being able to walk away with the *W* is victory. It means that I have earned a spot with a superstar, I have held my own. It is super sweet when I have pushed my opponent to a new height.

Oh, and it is not because I am Mr. Nice Guy. Nope. I just know that to focus on edging out the competition is so unimaginative. How silly to define your success by the limits of another. I had one sales manager who constantly preached about defeating the opposition. This fella had mounds of muscle but not a lick of sense. It was no surprise to me that he only held onto the role for three months. Triumph is about soaring. I want you to go out and set the bar. A favorite teacher of ours often said, "There is first, then there's everyone else."

This book is designed to bring you closer to realizing your own aspirations. In these pages, I have attempted to bare my soul and pour out my most helpful lessons. I truly hope you flourish as a result. Please let me hear from you, learn of your successes, and find ways to support your endeavors. Mostly, I yearn for you to support one another.

In conclusion, as you close these pages, I implore you to bask in your ambitions as you stroll enjoying a gorgeous walk.

I am going to do the same. Mine will be along the shore, perhaps you will be on a mountaintop, deep in a forest, or even in a city park.

As I ramble along the sand, I am likely to encounter one of my favorite animals, a horseshoe crab. They are magnificent. I love when a tourist runs in from a beach comb exclaiming "look at this 'prehistoric' creature I found." They are correct; horseshoe crabs have changed little over the past three hundred million years. Additionally, I am fascinated by their value to scientific research largely because of their copper-based blue blood. It breaks my heart that these glorious beings are in many ways endangered.

So, I love every chance I get to walk the beach flipping any horseshoe crabs as necessary. The tide often recedes too quickly, leaving them on dry land, flipped onto their heavy protective shells and unable to correct course. I am moved. I too know what it is like to be flat on my back, hopeless by the weight of my own choices, and stuck...and I believe most moms and entrepreneurs know that experience too.

Fortunately, I was often assisted in those situations and thus have three things to say to all those caring people who helped me: First, thank you for lifting me, flipping my perspective, and leading me to safety. Second, I am sorry I snapped my claws at you when all you were trying to do was help. Third, and most excitingly, I now know your joy of helping others succeed. The exhilaration of seeing someone achieve their goal is like none other. Magnifying that joy and stretching myself to help you was the driving factor behind this book. Thank you for motivating me in that way.

Acknowledgments

When Quarantine said I couldn't have you to my house for coffee, I decided to invite you into my heart for connection. So, YOU, readers, are the first "person" I want to thank. Hundreds of you emailed to say you purchased this book on pre-sale (yes...pre-sales happen before final edits which is why I get to write this). How could you have so much faith? How could you be so kind? I don't know, but I do know that I appreciate you.

My husband, Jeff Isaac, without whom this book and our stable lives would not exist. I love you and I treasure how you always bring a wonderful and different perspective to my stories and lessons.

My kids, the ultimate teachers. Savannah, Robert, and William, you are each uniquely funny, kind, smart, patient, curious, and interesting. I could never describe you in a sentence. Actually, I only scratch the surface with more than 49,000 words. I am certain that the world is better for your presence. Being your mom is my greatest joy.

My parents, Bill and Barb Strickland. You taught me about dreams and hard work. Your sixty-plus year love affair spills out in endless ways onto me and others.... Thank you for daily dedication and worldly wisdom. Mostly, thank you for leaving a trail of happiness and hilarious stories.

My sister, Betsy, and the Pagatpatan family. We launched our adult lives nearly 8,000 miles apart in Hawaii and Germany. Choosing to raise our families together was the best decision I have ever made. Thank you and Arnold for your continuous love and support for me, the kids, my work, and literally everything! Noa, Summer, and Grant, you fill our hearts and days with inspiration, companionship, love, and fun!

My brother, Bill, and his whole family. I especially treasure our beach walks.

The father of my children, Chris, and the entire Wray family. I am forever grateful for the children we welcomed to the world. I appreciate the spirit of adventure you brought to family decisions like moving to Munich, raising children on Daufuskie Island, and house swapping. Oma, thank you for always selecting the best books, activities, and intellectual field trips for me and the kids.

Laura Ferry Kelly, you define bestie like no other.

Juwan Platt, Donny Slater, and Keith Morgan, thank you for your magic wand you call a camera. Kait Lance, you rock the social. Kelly Foley is a perfect publicist. Jess Telmanik taught me about bookplates.

Finally, I am grateful for this opportunity. Soon Yu opened a door and CEO Anthony Ziccardi welcomed the call and my proposal. Thank you for making me an author.